ADVANCE PRAISE

"David Montesano has written a masterful book on how high school students can brand themselves in a way that will lead to winning more college acceptances. With top schools becoming more exclusive, getting the inside scoop on what excites college admission officers is invaluable. I highly recommend that parents and teenagers read this book."
   Lynn O'Shaughnessy, Education and Finance Writer, CBS Moneywatch

"Montesano expertly translates tried and tested strategies and marketing techniques into a "how to" get-into-the-college-of-your-choice guide. His techniques work. I know because my son got into 14 of the 15 schools he applied to, including his "reach" schools. Do not apply without reading this first!"
   John McLaughlin, Former CEO and Group President, Monster.com

What Families Are Saying About the Montesano Method

Ella V., attending Brown University (Ivy League)

David Montesano helped me organize and focus my application in order to present myself optimally. He and his writing specialists guided me through the essay-writing process and provided invaluable feedback on each essay. They were always extremely thorough and detailed in their feedback, and provided much-needed and knowledgeable perspective on all of my application writing. He also encouraged me to connect with professors in the departments of my interest, and with David's help, I was able to carry on dialogues with and secure supplementary recommendations from several professors at the schools I applied to. I truly believe that this networking made all the difference in getting me into my first-choice school. With College Match's help, I applied and was accepted Early Decision to my first choice—Brown!"

Aspen Jordan, admitted to Columbia University (Ivy League) and Williams College (Little Ivy)

David's advice helped me think strategically about my entrance essays and how to best fill out my applications and financial aid forms. When all was said and done, out of the ten schools I applied to, I was accepted to nine, including Columbia University, and waitlisted at one. Best of all, I received nearly full rides at almost every single school. Without the Montesano Method, I could never have gotten into the phenomenal college that I will be attending this fall.

Dennis Sisco, parent of student attending Tulane University (Southern Ivy)

Shelby was admitted to Emory. She received $96k in merit scholarships from Tulane, $88k from McDaniel, and $76k from Babson…sorry, I just couldn't resist crowing about my little girl.

Phoebe Merritt, attended Occidental College (West Coast Little Ivy)
I was accepted to every college I applied to including Tufts, Bates, and Macalester, with scholarships from University of Oregon ($4,000), University of Puget Sound ($12,000), Willamette University ($13,000), and Occidental College ($7,000)… your approach made a huge difference.

Milena Salmon, parent of Cornell University (Ivy League) student
Saying that David helped us would be to underestimate things. He did a fantastic job. My daughter started seeing a goal and together with David, we specified the steps required to reach it. Her grades improved, but most importantly, David noticed that she is a good writer and helped her unleash her creative potential and demonstrate to colleges her ability. She won several national awards and her stories were published in respected literary journals. Along with this, David helped us choose the right colleges and guided us through the entire application process. My daughter was accepted to some of the most selective colleges in the country: Bard, Sarah Lawrence and Cornell University. Some of the colleges (Whittier and Mills) gave her big merit-based scholarships. We definitely would not have had such a great choice of colleges if we had not worked with David.

Alex, accepted to graduate computer engineering programs at Cornell University (Ivy League) and Carnegie Mellon University
As a full-time professional, applying to a dozen top universities seemed daunting, but David's process helped me choose institutions that would be the best match for my interest and long-term goals. He assessed my overall strategy, guaranteeing that I would be satisfied with the outcome of these stressful months of preparation. While David and the team didn't directly make changes to my main application essay, they provided feedback and guidance, making sure I focused on my strengths and explained shortcomings in a positive light. My situation was unusual: I had a poor GPA, and yet I aspired to be part of some of the world's toughest graduate programs.

David was extremely available in our communications and was willing to go the extra mile to make sure I was happy with the results. He was even able to sleuth out a fantastic opportunity I had overlooked: I succeeded at entering the top-ranked graduate program in my field. I was actually able to turn down offers from the other top 5 schools in favor of my dream school. I might have gone down this path alone, but I didn't want to gamble with this important step toward my future career. David and College Match ensured my chances of getting in were as high as they could possibly be, and that success would be determined by the quality of my preparedness versus a roll of the dice.

BRAND U

4 Steps to the
College of Your Dreams

DAVID MONTESANO

Brand U: 4 Steps to the College of Your Dreams

Copyright © 2014 by David Montesano

PRINTED IN THE UNITED STATES OF AMERICA

Visit our website: www. BrandUBook.com

ISBN-13: 978-0-9904314-1-1

Published by: August Books

Cover design: Kristie Langone, 2 Faced Design LLC
Interior design: Adina Cucicov, Flamingo Designs

TABLE OF CONTENTS

INTRODUCTION

I GREW UP in the field of education with a father who worked as a learning disabilities researcher. My personal journey as an education consultant began with the marketing strategy work I performed for companies as a management and brand consultant. Although I found my corporate work intellectually stimulating, it was hard to build the satisfying personal connections I wanted, and I didn't feel as if I was making a difference in people's lives or helping them reach their goals.

Where I could make such an impact at the individual level was in the field of college admissions. The admissions process, I discovered, is stacked in colleges' favor, and I wanted to level the playing field. Taking the ideas that I had gained in the world of branding and marketing strategy, I sought to help students "tame the admissions dragon" in the same way that companies use branding and marketing strategy to reach their goals. Since 2001, my admissions consulting company, College Match, has given hundreds of families necessary strategies to help their children **find the right college**, **get accepted**, and **thrive once they're in**.

I began offering professional guidance in college admissions because I saw the need to empower families through many challenges of college admissions. I saw that undergraduate institutions held too much power in the process, and for the past seventeen years, I've worked to level the playing field.

As an education consultant, I travel around the country to meet with concerned parents. One day, I'm reassuring a high-powered CEO in Manhattan who's frantic that her daughter might not get into her alma mater, Harvard. Next, I'm working with a father in London who wants his twins to find the best universities, but isn't sure what "the best" means. Then I'm off to Seattle to visit a computer programmer concerned that her son isn't invested in his college future. College admission is an ever-increasing global concern.

As unique as each parent is, they all have this in common: they work diligently, dedicating their lives to making sure their children have the opportunities to grow into fulfilled and self-reliant adults, knowing that the foundation for future opportunities is a high-quality undergraduate experience.

Unfortunately, gaining access to the most prestigious schools has become enormously competitive, with students vying for a limited number of spots. The application process has become difficult and uncertain, even at the state universities, and dedicated, hardworking students are getting turned away.

In short, college admission is now a high-stakes affair, with no margin for error. Admissions officers take just 10-20 minutes to rate each application. In this scant time, acceptance or rejection is decided, and a child's future is sealed.

That's why I'm devoted to helping students make the most of this brief window of opportunity and put themselves in positions of high demand. With *Brand U*, I present you with the Montesano Method, a set of strategies with nearly two decades of incredible success. More than 96% of my students have gained acceptance to their first-choice schools, winning an average of $57,000 in merit aid over a four-year period. Beyond the admissions process, the Montesano Method enables students to build the skills, vision, and sense of purpose to not only get into college but to thrive while they're there, so that they're well-prepared to meet the challenges of life after they graduate.

At its core, the Montesano Method identifies and nurtures each student's "spark"—the talents and contributions he or she alone can offer the world. Once the spark is lit, it reveals a sense of purpose and vision which guides students toward the college that's right for them. Then, using our Brand tool, the centerpiece of the Montesano Method, we create a statement of value: a portrait of each child's unique attributes and strengths. This statement leaves an indelible impression on admissions officers, ensuring that your son or daughter is not just one of hundreds of applicants, but a student the college is eager to welcome as one of their own.

I hope you enjoy *Brand U*. I'm confident it will help you find—and get into—the college of your dreams.

TWO APPROACHES TO COLLEGE

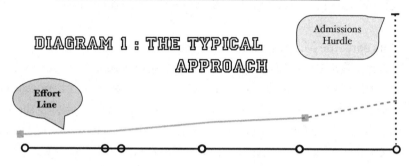

DIAGRAM 1 : THE TYPICAL APPROACH

Part I	**Part II**	**Part III**	**Part IV**
Action: Prep	Prep	Selection	Application
Grade: 9th & 10th	10th & 11th	Late 11th	Early 12th
Typical activities and clubs, (or not)	Typical Activities and Clubs, (or not)	College Selection via typical methods	Basic Prep and Strategy

Part I: Too few students find and embrace their core interests and talents, and as a result, end up choosing extracurriculars by conformity, to please peers, parents, or coaches.

Part II: Students pursue activities and clubs out of a sense of duty, because they *have to*. Since these efforts feel tedious, students waste valuable time avoiding activities they don't enjoy instead of pursuing what they love doing. Consequently, many students get to the college selection process with no real sense of what their strongest skills and passions are.

Part III: College selection feels overwhelming. As a result, parents and students look to superficials like magazine rankings, sports games, and party reputation, and make hasty choices that lead to poor college matches. Poor college matches lead to financial waste and personal frustration as students drop out, transfer, or fail to use their education to its fullest.

Part IV: Applications get filled out without a strategy. Students send in their applications, hoping for the best, not realizing that their applications are just one among thousands. When applications don't stand out, students get rejected, miss out on scholarship aid, and suffer a feeling of disappointment, all of which is completely avoidable with the right strategy...

DIAGRAM 2 : THE BRAND U APPROACH

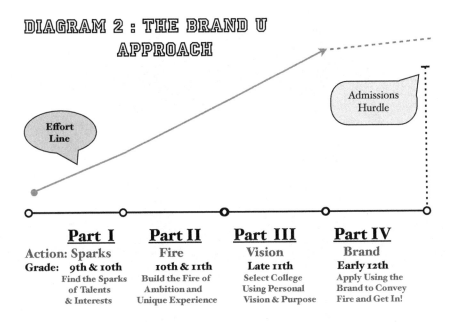

Part I	**Part II**	**Part III**	**Part IV**
Action: Sparks	Fire	Vision	Brand
Grade: 9th & 10th	10th & 11th	Late 11th	Early 12th
Find the Sparks of Talents & Interests	Build the Fire of Ambition and Unique Experience	Select College Using Personal Vision & Purpose	Apply Using the Brand to Convey Fire and Get In!

Part I: Brand U guides students to identify their unique sparks. Students locate the interests and strengths that make them who they are, thus beginning a path of self-discovery and a meaningful journey into adulthood.

Part II: Brand U shows students how to build their unique sparks into a fire of vision and purpose. Students pursue growth experiences and gain the confidence and self-awareness to thrive through the challenges of college admissions and beyond.

Part III: Brand U helps students brush aside selection pitfalls, like magazine rankings, sports teams, and party reputation. Instead, Brand U gives students a streamlined process to locate the right college match.

Part IV: Brand U guides students through the challenging application process, empowering them with the time-tested tool of the branded statement of unique identity, a unified theme, which conveys the fire of their vision and leaves an indelible impression of maturity on admissions officers. By standing out, students get in and increase their chances of merit aid.

PARENTS

SECTION

PARENTS, THIS SECTION is for you.

After working closely with parents for close to two decades, I've seen the effort and sacrifice that comes with raising a child. Through every high and low of childhood, you've felt the joy of your child's transformations—from first smiles and first words to the first days of kindergarten, elementary school, and junior high—all with the devotion of helping your student thrive.

That is the spirit that inspires this book.

Love and hard work leads us to the greatest transformation of all, the gateway into adulthood: college. To get there, kids need help. Even the most independent adolescents need guidance and perspective. As a parent, you've seen the challenges and pitfalls of life. You know success stories of those who develop their talents and passions, and you know the trials of those who don't.

In the sections that follow, we'll guide you through the process of preparing your student for college selection, admissions and beyond, working in a step-by-step collaboration that will empower your student to flourish through the challenges to come.

BRAND U

the path ahead

SPARKS—We help your child find his or her unique talents and interests to get excited about the process ahead.

FIRE—We ignite the inspiration, helping your child find unique and transformative experiences that will instill a vision and purpose for the future.

VISION—We navigate the complex process of college selection to pinpoint the undergraduate experience that matches your child's values, hopes, and ambitions, and offers the life he or she wants to have.

BRAND—We empower you through the admissions process with the time-tested tool that stokes the fire of ambition and conveys to admissions officers how your student offers a unique value that few other students can.

PART I

SPARKS

Fire

Vision

Brand

1

CREATING SPARKS:

the need for method

COLLEGE CAN BE approached in two ways:

- The *adult* fashion, using a step-by-step strategy to meet the tough challenges of preparation, selection, and admission head-on in an inspired way.
- The *adolescent* fashion, avoiding the tough challenges with hasty preparation, procrastination, and conforming to what others do.

The college experience, and the many decades of life that follow, are very much determined by the approach to college as it is by college itself. College begins long before students arrives on campus, even before they fill out applications or select schools.

College begins now, while your child is still in high school. The actions and intentions of today create the life your child will lead in the years to come. As a parent, you've spent years of steady dedication and sacrifice to give your child a rewarding life.

We realize that time is limited but you can still play the pivotal role of helping your student grasp the magnitude of this moment and the importance of approaching college with a method.

the need for method: college selection

Most high school students, without guidance, will take an adolescent approach to college. They'll choose by what matters to them in the moment, the thrill of football games or amazing parties or the prestige of a magazine ranking, not realizing that there are far more profound elements that must come into play. As a result, many students select schools without thinking through what they want out of college and where college will take them—a choice which is in many ways a blind leap that lands them in the frustration and regret of dropping out, transferring, and being disappointed at school, all at the cost of lost years and tens, if not hundreds of thousands of dollars.

The Montesano Method makes sure that doesn't happen.

Through a series of sure-footed steps, *Brand U* guides students through a process of self-discovery, working organically from each student's unique talents and interests. Through experience with the Brand U method, students build a fire of vision that helps students see where they want college to take them. As a result, when the time for choosing comes, students can pinpoint the undergraduate experience best suited for them.

the need for method: gaining admission

Students have a million things on their minds. Every day brings a constant flux of expectations from parents, friends, peers, coaches, and teachers, just to name a few. With so much to worry about, college preparation can often seem like just another chore.

Out of a sense of duty, students might peruse some websites and attend the required test-prep classes, but ultimately, the applications get filled out with fingers crossed. With admissions becoming more and more competitive by the year, this approach is like a roll of the dice.

Admission comes. Or it doesn't. Either way, this is a passive, disempowered approach, and we believe a child's future is far too valuable to leave things to chance.

Therefore, *Brand U* builds off each student's inner fire and sense of purpose to forge an identity that is conveyed to admissions boards through the Brand, a time-tested tool that can increase a student's chance of admission by as much 92 percent over the national average.

Twice as many schools, twice as many options, all because of a little front-loaded effort.

the need for method: performance in college

An astounding number of college students don't graduate in four years: over 40%!

Without the support system of home, college can be a time of regression from high school successes to a time of wandering and grasping at external expectations of success for many young people. Many students leave school disappointed with their experience, and approach the "real world" feeling unprepared, with deep anxiety about what they are supposed to "do with their lives."

These unpleasant realities can be curtailed with a method that makes sure that the transformation into adulthood begins long before the weight of college graduation sets in.

Brand U offers parents and students a fun and rewarding collaboration that will help students maximize their college experience and enter the real world with poise and momentum.

We begin this collaboration by exploring what your hopes and intentions are for the journey ahead. Take the time to express to your hopes for your child, and listen closely to what your child envisions, observing ways you can lend support.

Exercise: Hopes & Intentions

(30 minutes)

Goal: To explore your hopes and intentions for the journey your child will take into adulthood.

Instructions: Write all your hopes and dreams for your student, for college, and after college. How do you imagine your child leading a happy and fulfilled life in the decades to come? Write whatever comes to mind.

Think Like An Admissions Officer
Uniqueness

You're an admissions officer at a major university. For three very intense months, you spend somewhere between six and twelve hours each day reading applications—hundreds of them—from nice, well-meaning kids, and you have somewhere between 10 and 20 minutes to decide their fate.

In that time, you have to figure out who the student is, what makes her special, and what unique value she can offer the university. Unfortunately, as you flip through the files, you find the same molds repeating themselves, an endless succession of honors students and varsity athletes, math club members and science team leaders, all with good track records, but with little to help you distinguish what's special.

Your vision blurs. You yawn, stretch, and toss another file into the 50/50 pile.

You reach for another, wondering how much more you can take, when suddenly, you wake from your stupor, reading about a student with unique promise—an unusual combination of passion and talent who has constructed a rock-solid picture of who she is, what she loves, and what she wants out of life.

Her unique experience will add value to your university in ways that no other student can, and her knowledge about your school proves how vested she is in creating her future. You feel a tingling, a thrill of pride as you place her in the acceptance pile, giving her a springboard into a promising future.

It's moments like these that make the job worthwhile.

2

LOCATING SPARKS:
value and uniqueness

COLLEGES GET THOUSANDS of applications each year, and it's their job to decide whose life stories are most compelling and most deserving of acceptance. Admissions officers get a fleeting glimpse of who your child really is. They see test scores and grades. They note the extracurriculars and they read the essays. They take into consideration the experiences and achievements, and they make a story about who your child is.

The challenge is that after reading thousands of applications, admissions officers see the same roles played out over and over. The stories blend into repeated types, none of which stand out. Therefore, the first thing College Match staff do when we meet with students is to find out what they care about most, what they've excelled at, and what has given them a sense of pride.

Our goal is to locate the sparks, strengths, and passions that can ignite a fire of transformative growth. The sooner students grasp these sparks, the sooner they know who they are and what they need to pursue in order to get what they want in life.

Many students learn to *survive* high school by conforming to other people's expectations, by fitting the molds and labels that will get them the approval and sense of value they seek. From an admissions standpoint, conforming is the opposite of what a student wants to do. Colleges look for students who know who they are and what they love. If a young person spends their time trying to conform, standing out in the application process is very hard to do.

It's hard to be unique, and in certain environments—where young people face bullying or intimidation—being different can seem downright scary. Yet individuality is the key to getting into the right college and thriving thereafter. That's why your child needs your support, to make sure he catches his sparks.

As admissions consultants, we often take the role of guiding students toward their strengths as the first steps in the journey to college. In addition to working with your child to discover his unique talents and interests, it's helpful to meet with mentors, teachers, coaches, counselors, and other adults your student admires.

Exercise: Finding the Sparks

(30 minutes)

Goal: To help students recognize their favorite growth experiences, and where they get a strong sense of pride.

Instructions: Working with your child, discuss the experiences, activities, teams, clubs, hobbies, that have given your child the greatest sense of satisfaction. For each experience, explore what these experiences offered in terms of skills, lessons learned, and feats accomplished.

Exercise: Mentor Interviews

(30 minutes)

Goal: To create mentor connections to support of your child's unique talents and interests.

Instructions: Make time to meet with your child's favorite mentors, (teachers, coaches, counselors, employers, etc.) Interview them to find out what they feel are your child's strengths and talents, and where they see opportunities for your child to grow.

BRAND U

the path ahead

- **Finding the transformative experiences** to instill a sense of vision and purpose for the future (**FIRE**)

- **Developing a strong vision for the future** that will guide your child through the college selection process (**VISION**)

- **Creating the Brand statement** that conveys the unique value your child offers a college (**BRAND**)

PART II

Sparks
FIRE
Vision
Brand

IN THE SPARKS section, we looked at ways to kindle your child's unique talents and interests. Now, we take those sparks and ignite a fire of vision and purpose and create clarity and momentum for the college selection and admissions process. There are great challenges ahead, but when young people light the fire of their unique identity, they become driven, fueled by inspiration toward amazing possibilities.

The world puts people into categories. In high school, kids get typecast as jocks, preps, hippies, cheerleaders, nerds, thespians, and band geeks. Our goal is to help students realize that they define their own lives, that by pursuing their talents and interests through unique paths and transformative experiences, they can build strengths and passions into identities they can develop in college and throughout their lives.

FINDING FIRE:

life intentions

TO MAXIMIZE YOUR student's opportunities moving forward, we want to look at the intentions that will fuel his or her growth. We dig into the hopes and dreams to find the wells of ambition that inspire the best your child has to offer. In the table below, examples of hopes and dreams are listed at the top, and below each one, the surface ambitions versus the deeper ambitions.

Table 4.1—Example Life Goals of Students

	Professional singer	*Famous Software Developer*	*Nobel Prize Winner—Science*
Surface Ambition	To be famous	To be rich and powerful	To be remembered and celebrated
Underlying Social Ambition	To make people happy	To make people's lives easier	To help the world in some major way
Underlying Personal Ambition	To perform	To invent, make dreams a reality	To be a leader in scientific discovery

These are natural ambitions students often have, so let's probe the underlying intentions:

Being a **professional singer** is appealing in many ways, such as for the pleasure of being sought after and famous. However, the desire for fame is hardly a good motivator (or nearly everyone would be famous). Looking more closely, we find that beneath fame there are heartfelt desires—to make people happy and to express creativity through performance. These intentions can be lived out in many positive ways and can bring great satisfaction, whether on the stage or off.

Being a **successful software developer** would allow one to be rich and powerful; however, that desire hardly achieves anything, or else we'd all be billionaires. On the other hand, the ambition to improve people's lives and to pursue an invention can spark a journey to success that can take many different forms and drive unique growth opportunities.

Being a **Nobel Prize winner in science** sounds appealing for the honor of being remembered and celebrated, but on a deeper and more meaningful level, this desire is rooted in the twin ambitions of helping the world in some major way and pursuing scientific discovery, both of which can be developed in many different ways.

Following the examples above, collaborate with your child to uncover the deep personal and service ambitions that underlie his or her hopes and dreams. These core ambitions are the intentions that we'll use to drive the experiences to come.

Exercise: Fueling the Sparks

(30 minutes)

Goal: To locate each student's deep ambitions.

Instructions: Work with your child to fill out the table below.

	Life Hope #1 _____	Life Hope #2 _____	Life Hope #3 _____
Surface Ambition			
Deep Service Ambition			
Deep Personal Ambition			

IGNITING FIRE:

transformative paths

ONCE UPON A time, admission to elite colleges was all but assured by high grades and strong test scores. Nowadays, high marks will barely get you in the door. Once students clear the hurdles of GPA and SAT, extracurriculars make or break their chances.

Colleges want to see high-level development and commitment. They want to see students who have identified their strengths and propelled themselves forward with drive and intensity. Robin Mamlet, the former Dean of Admission and Financial Aid at Stanford, has described **"academic excitement"** as the common attribute displayed by students who gained acceptance to elite colleges.

What others calls academic excitement, we call **fire**. When fired up about their future, students no longer approach classes and extracurriculars as dutiful efforts to stock a resume. They're driven by inspiration and the burning curiosity of self-discovery and self-determination.

Fire is the drive that takes your child's talents and interests to the next level of skills and passions. Fire is what gives your child a vision of the life she wants to pursue and to convey confidence and purpose to admissions boards. Fire will carry your student into college, maximize undergraduate experiences, and provide momentum for meeting the real world with a sense of maturity.

This process isn't about meeting external expectations or comparing your child against others. It's about your child finding and engaging in distinct, well-fitting experiences to find a sense of purpose and fulfillment. For nearly two decades, I've helped young people prepare for college by encouraging the four paths of growth and maturation that colleges look for in applications:

- Leadership
- Entrepreneurship
- Service
- Creativity

If your child hasn't won a major award, been published, or started a business, don't be discouraged. All students have a unique talent and passion, a clear fire that will naturally emerge as they pursue their talents and interests.

I say this with certainty because I have seen hundreds of young people discover their hidden talents and do extraordinary things once they found their inner fire. I've included some of their stories here for inspiration.

As you read, remember that when these students first started working with us, they felt as uncertain about the road ahead as your child might feel.

transformative paths: leadership

Colleges want students who have shown a capacity to lead. While colleges appreciate seeing leadership at school, they're most impressed by leadership experiences that don't fit a pre-existing mold, roles that individual students develop through their own initiative, using original ideas and out-of-the box thinking.

Joseph from Phoenix, Arizona

Sparks: Love of tennis, outgoing, selfless
Igniting Fire: Unique leadership

Joseph came to us as a sophomore in high school, a good student and competitive tennis player in Phoenix, Arizona, but with little development of other skills. Together, we sought ways that he could use his passion for tennis to develop skills of leadership and encouraged him to look for ways he could serve the needs of his community. In the spring of 10th grade, Joseph contacted his local Boys and Girls Club and learned that Phoenix had few summer programs to help inner-city youth stay out of trouble, and so Joseph created a plan for a tennis clinic for low-income children in the area.

Working with his parents, he visited local pro shops, got sponsors for his clinic and acquired used racquets and balls for the kids. Next, he worked with the local Boys and Girls club to secure tennis courts. That summer, Joseph's camp grew in popularity, increasing from just eight kids the first week to fifty by the end of the summer. We urged Joseph to take his success and scale it upwards, so during his junior year he wrote a handbook on how to start tennis clinics in other areas. Then the following summer, Joseph expanded his inner-city tennis program to two other cities across the country.

Discovered Brand: Community Leader, Entrepreneur

----

transformative paths: entrepreneurship

While the idea of starting a business or nonprofit may seem daunting, experience has shown that once a young person put a plan on paper for a good idea, the doors of possibility fly open.

There is something undeniably inspiring about a young person taking initiative and starting something from scratch. Without fail, the students I've worked with have found no shortage of enthusiastic supporters to help them realize their vision. The process starts with creating a concept and learning how to draft a business proposal.

For parents, entrepreneurship offers the great satisfaction of collaborating with kids to build a business venture. Creating a unique venture demands individuality, responsibility, and maturity, but it's also a lot of fun.

The hardest part is just getting started.

Ali from Santa Clara, California

Sparks: Compassion, love of people
Igniting Fire: Entrepreneurship

We began working with Ali as a ninth grader. Unsure of her talents, she had sincere interest in her family's Romanian background. The following summer, she volunteered at an orphanage in Bucharest. Gradually, she became aware of her sense of compassion and desire to help. She was so taken by the children's needs that when she returned to her high school in Silicon Valley, she got her friends to help her organize a nonprofit to raise awareness about the children's hardships and how financial support could have a meaningful, long-lasting impact on these children.

In the subsequent years she held fundraisers, which illustrated the management skills, organization, and publicity that she had gained. Meanwhile, she brought awareness to her community and raised over $20,000 to improve living conditions for the Romanian children in need.

Discovered Brand: NGO Founder

----

transformative paths: service

Colleges value service and philanthropy, particularly when students expand beyond school and religious-based activities and create a unique role for themselves. Volunteering for a worthy cause is a good start, but don't stop there. Use it as a springboard for developing your child's unique talents, interests, and vision.

That's exactly what Peter did. As you'll see, his story illustrates an incredible burst in confidence by a young person who began with no idea of what he was capable of and ended up surpassing his wildest expectations.

Peter from Berkeley, California

Sparks: Love of art, creative, inspired
Igniting Fire: Unique service

When we started working with Peter, he expressed few interests except for drawing and designing models in his backyard. His parents were anxious about his lack of focus at school, and so we began working with Peter to explore ways that he could use his sparks to help others. By chance, Peter's father had contacts with a charitable NGO that built homes in Guatemala.

Peter applied for a work visa while in 10th grade and spent the next summer in Guatemala learning how the homes were designed and built. When he returned home, he spent the school year applying his passion to learning blueprint design. The following summer, he was able to implement the plans that he'd created, and he watched his designs become homes for needy Guatemalans. As a result, Peter gained great confidence and satisfaction, and won entrance into Washington University's premiere architectural program.

Discovered Brand: Architect

----

transformative paths: creativity

As the word 'creativity' suggests, there are countless ways your student can develop imaginative talent. Admissions boards are always won over by creativity, particularly when students apply their unique talents to fill needs and niches in new and original ways. Time and again, the students we've worked with have channeled the most unusual ideas into impressive accomplishments, as George managed to do. Here's his story:

George from Sacramento, CA

Sparks: Lyrical talent, love of music
Igniting Fire: Unique creativity

George, a junior from Sacramento, came to us with a great deal of uncertainty over what talents or skills he could possibly offer a university. A creative spirit, he loathed the idea of competition. As a result, he wasn't interested in extracurriculars, and in fact, had few interests beyond hip hop music. Instead of forcing him into fields he wasn't interested in, we encouraged George to pursue his passion for hip hop in new and creative ways.

His sophomore year, while studying for the SATs, he noted how many of his fellow students struggled with pre-calculus. So the following summer, he wrote, recorded, and using his home equipment, produced hip hop songs that taught fundamentals of calculus in a way that his fellow students could relate to. His efforts won recognition at his school and became an online sensation popular with schools across the country.

Discovered Brand: Music Producer

- -

Using your child's deep ambitions, explore which unique paths feel right for igniting your student's sparks. Let your imagination take over. Don't worry if the idea seems daunting or unrealistic. In fact, the path requires leaving comfort zones and risking failure, but the payoff for doing so, even the lessons of failure, are well worth the effort.

By taking small steps and working with a plan, momentum will build on itself. Let our examples remind you that anything is possible, and that the anxiety of starting something new quickly turns to the thrill of discovery. Igniting fire just takes the first step.

Exercise: Igniting the Sparks

(30 minutes)

Goal: To find inspiring paths of development.

Instructions: Brainstorm fun and creative ways your child can apply his or her interests and talents through leadership, creativity, service, or entrepreneurship.
   Discuss the best ideas, and once your child has picked an inspiring option, collaborate on ways to move forward, seeking advice from mentors, and writing a plan.

5

BUILDING FIRE:

transformative experience

IN CHAPTER 3, we explored ways to set your child's sparks on fire through unique paths of transformation. Now we move forward, exploring the specific types of unique experiences that help our students develop into formidable admissions candidates.

As we discussed before, high schools across the country segregate kids into types: the math kids, the science kids, the jocks, the popular ones, and the squares. The purpose of this chapter is to help you and your child realize that regardless of whatever labels peers or teachers might want to apply to your student, this is his time to pursue his deepest drive. This is his time to define his sense of purpose and the vision of the life he wants to live.

Over the past two decades, we've found that the following six types of experience offer students extraordinary opportunities for growth and are excellent ways to further define passions and skills:

- University programs
- Personalized employment
- Competitions and scholarships
- Research
- Personalized international experiences
- Publishing and performance

transformative experience: university programs

Participation in a summer program at a university has many benefits. First, it can show experience to committed learning away from parents, offering students a chance to learn under highly-regarded professors and observe the atmosphere of collegiate life. It can also prepare them for development outside the familiar world of their hometown and school. Moreover, most universities offer higher-level programs that can both expose a student to collegiate-level instruction or shore up weak spots in one's GPA. Most major universities offer such programs, many of them with merit-based scholarships.

Jenny from Manhattan, New York

Sparks: Writing Skills, persistence
Building Fire: University program

When we met Jenny, she was a sophomore and an aspiring poet. With this in mind, we urged her to submit her work to various summer programs, and she won entrance into the prestigious University of Iowa's Young Writer's Workshop, where she spent the next summer developing her work under published authors.

With their guidance, she returned home with a polished portfolio that she was able to submit to multiple competitions. The following school year, she continued her development as a writer, traveling cross-country to deliver poetry readings in Ithaca, NY and at Hugo House in Seattle. That spring, she was awarded a National Scholastic

Award for creative writing. The subsequent year, with these credits, she gained admission to the highly-regarded English programs at Cornell and Sarah Lawrence as a result of her work.

Discovered Brand: Published Author

----

transformative experience: employment

Getting a good job in an area of strong interest is a great way to develop skills, confidence, and a sense of purpose. What you don't want is for your child to settle for random jobs. Time is ticking, and the skills that she doesn't develop today will have to wait until tomorrow. The job that puts students on a path to self-discovery and development will propel them that much further in life, expanding horizons and creating excitement about the future.

Bill from Honolulu, Hawaii

Sparks: Positivity, leadership
Building Fire: Unique employment

Bill began volunteering at a local YMCA in 9th grade, and by his junior year, he had become a student athletic director, organizing leagues and teaching kids in after-school programs the rules of basketball and indoor soccer. During this time, one of the kids, Jack, caught his attention because of the hard time he had following directions. After contacting the family, Bill learned that the boy suffered from an acute case of autism.

While working with Bill on his college development, we advised him to research autism, and Bill got in touch with learning disability experts to find out ways to help Jack. Over time, he became a coach and mentor to Jack and other children who had learning challenges. The result was that his college essays revealed a high degree of maturity and compassion, and won him admission and merit award offers into Haverford, Whitman, and Lewis and Clark.

Discovered Identity: Community Leader, Mentor

----

transformative experience: competition

Every year, thousands of awards and scholarships are given out to qualified young people across the country in various fields of academic competition. Even just applying for scholarships can create opportunities for development and constructive validation of your child's unique talents. Win or lose, your child can aspire to ever higher levels of achievement. Of course, winning never hurts!

Paula from Florence, Italy

Sparks: Love of science, courage
Building Fire: Unique competition

When we met Paula, we asked her which adults she admired, and she described her grandfather, a doctor. From a young age, he'd captivated her imagination with his descriptions of surgery and healing the sick. As she entered high school, Paula discovered a passion for science—physiology in particular—so we encouraged her to pursue ways to explore these areas outside of school.

The summer after 10th grade, she worked at a local blood bank, which led to her applying and being accepted to Oxford University Hospital as an intern her junior year. While there, she worked directly under doctors studying links between cancer and red meat consumption. From her work, she drafted up a paper that she researched, developed, and submitted to a state science fair competition. The recognition she received from winning that competition gave a much-needed boost to her confidence and helped solidify her vision of becoming a doctor. It also helped her gain admissions to Tufts University in Boston.

Discovered Brand: Medical Researcher

----

transformative experience: research

Pursuing research while in high school allows students to get a head start on their collegiate future by working closely with professional mentors in a variety of fields, from science to journalism, just to name a few.

Conducting research teaches technical skills and discipline that push students' talents to a higher level, creates legitimacy in the eyes of admission boards, and can help your child focus on specific life ambitions. To prospective colleges, research displays academic dedication and a willingness to push learning to a higher level, and it can serve to both augment academic accomplishment and shore up weaknesses in GPA or test scores.

Tariq from Los Angeles, California

Sparks: Passion for politics and human rights, strong writing skills
Building Fire: Conducting research

Tariq was a sophomore in high school when we began working with him. Because of his core interests and talents, we urged him to study political science through a university program. He was accepted to Harvard's summer program, and chose to study the complex political situation in Pakistan. At Harvard, he began to amass research under a doctorate-level professor, who guided him towards writing a policy piece on the Barelvi movement in Pakistan. With the help of our in-house writing advisor, Tariq developed his work, which won attention from the department chair of Harvard's Islamic Studies program, a noteworthy accomplishment that solidified his confidence and earned him acceptance to Columbia and the University of Chicago.

Discovered Brand: Political Scholar

----

transformative experience: unique international work/study

International work and study are fantastic routes for personal growth. Students expand their horizons through immersion into new cultures, new languages, and the discovery that the world is far greater and more complex than ever before imagined.

International experience has to be unique, however.

Every year, thousands of well-meaning students venture abroad in volunteer programs, tutoring in orphanages, and cleaning up after floods. While structured programs are a good place to start, they don't often provide a unique experience, and for that reason they fail to impress colleges during the admissions process. Colleges simply see too many applicants with the same experiences.

The problem with many programs is that they are pre-planned and self-contained. Students get little opportunity to show initiative or to branch out beyond the group of students very similar to themselves. Rather than developing their own unique talents, they end up playing a role much like back home. They go far away, only to reenter life back at home the same way as they left.

Colleges want to see transformative growth from international experiences. If a student volunteers at an orphanage in Mexico, colleges want to see her take that experience to the next level and uses her creativity and people skills to start a nonprofit or hold fundraisers to raise awareness.

If a student ventures to Thailand to work on flood relief with an NGO, colleges want to see him use his interest in engineering to develop a flood evacuation plan or do field research that restores the quality of drinking water. We find that international experiences help students when the experience serves as a catalyst for growth, not as an end unto itself. If your child is interested in going abroad, work with her to set up a plan for how to best utilize and develop skills and interests while abroad and how to take the experience further upon returning home.

Malika from Portland, Oregon

Sparks: A passion for social sciences and international affairs
Building Fire: Unique international work

We met Malika as a sophomore. Her parents were doctors and she had extended family living in Africa. During trips abroad, she experienced first-hand the HIV epidemic in Uganda and came back determined to help. With our encouragement, she took courses at a local college and received guidance to begin a study on methods that could decrease infection rates, which gained recognition from a national online journal and attention from a Pan-African conference. Her work helped solidify her passion and authenticity as an agent of change and service, helping her gain admission and a merit-based scholarship to Occidental College, where she now majors in Diplomacy and World Affairs, in addition to interning at the United Nations in New York.

Discovered Brand: International Aid Worker

P
A
R
E
N
T
S

transformative experience: performance/publishing

In a highly competitive world, students who can publish or perform their talents stand out. It takes dedication, courage, and poise to build one's talents to the level of recognition and place them before the judgment of an audience.

Student writers and artists can profile their work in various publications—newspapers, magazines, and online journals, from the local to state to national levels—and fortunately, there has never been a better time to self-publish. From Cafepress.com to Lulu.com, students can publish, print, and customize their work to a professional level.

Social media is a great way to publish a student's ideas and highlight accomplishments. Your student may choose to publish his or her written work digitally using Kindle or iBooks, blogs like WordPress, or social media platforms like YouTube and SlideShare. Digital expression also makes it easy to track performance. For example, using digital media platforms, your student can measure the number of downloads, reviews, or sales.

Many college applications ask at what level a student's accomplishments occurred—local, regional or national. We highly recommend our artistic clients compile a portfolio. Once completed, they can collaborate with fellow artists and set up an exhibition in the community, featuring a series of a dozen or more of their best works. The experience of "professionalizing" their art before a live audience will take your child's talent and passion to a higher level.

Student actors, musicians, and performers also have many creative options. We've helped young people join performance groups and collectives. If your child can't find a venue to perform in, it's all the better if he begins his own. He'll get the thrill of learning production firsthand by staging and arranging performances, talent nights, and other celebrations that create a sense of community and help others share their voice. Your student's mentors and teachers will be glad to assist.

As with other experiences, it's fine if your student performs within a school program, but she will grow exponentially by venturing out and creating her own unique plan and performance vision.

Erika from Brooklyn, New York

Sparks: Creative passion, imagination, and dedication
Building Fire: Unique performance

When we interviewed Erika, we uncovered that her greatest ambition in life was "to express her creativity through the arts." Her interests revolved around writing and theater, so we encouraged her to try writing a play. With guidance from her English teacher and writing coaches, she wrote out a script based on her life in New York City.

After writing several drafts, her play was performed at her high school, and to her surprise, the play was widely accepted in her community as a great work. With this boost of confidence, she decided to take her story to a larger audience. Enlisting the support of her parents, friends, and fellow drama classmates, she held a fundraiser to get her classmates and herself to Scotland the following year. After a year of organizing, they performed their piece and won recognition at the Edinburgh Fringe Festival.

Discovered Brand: Playwright and Theatrical Producer

Advice for
Transformative Experience

- If interested in the health field, consider internships in hospitals, and find health needs in the community, determining the organizations that bring awareness, outreach, and support. Start there, and take it even further through research opportunities and creating your own outreach group in your school or community.
- If interested in science, look for research opportunities via projects and look for competitions and scholarships in math, engineering, and technology. Bridge and university programs can often be a great place to find mentoring and research opportunities. Another outlet is finding ways to apply special skills in math, finance, computer science, or engineering to social needs.
- If interested in finance or business, consider opportunities for entrepreneurship, and seek guidance from mentors, look for opportunities to create a business or philanthropy, draft a proposal, and seek funding.
- If interested in sports, find ways to use your passion for athletics to help the underserved in your community, through youth programs, coaching, and leadership.
- If interested in the arts, explore ways to build a portfolio of your work through film, writing, and performance. Team up with others to create supportive environments, performance nights, gallery showings, and offer creative services to help others in distinct ways.
- If interested in international relations and foreign cultures, explore unique work and study opportunities abroad. Before you go, be sure to create a plan, and afterwards, a statement, research paper, or journalistic expression detailing what you learned, to be submitted for publication.

Exercise: Building Fire

(30 minutes)

Goal: To help your child create transformative growth experiences.

Instructions:

1. **Discussion**—Collaborate with your child to brainstorm unique experiences that will build upon your child's unique talents, interests, and ambitions (come up with two or three favorites).

   - Summer university bridge programs
   - Unique employment
   - Academic competitions and scholarships
   - Research projects
   - International experience
   - Publishing
   - Portfolio development

2. **Research**—Once your child has a few favorite options, work together to research options via mentors, online searches, and word of mouth. The idea is to find experiences that build naturally from your child's strongest interests and talents so that the experience will be a springboard for further growth. *(Advice: If your child can't envision wanting to build on the experience, keep looking.)*

3. **Planning**—Encourage imagination and have fun. Help your child create a plan for making the experience dynamic and exciting.

INSPIRING FIRE:

personal triumphs

LIFE IN HIGH school can be tough.

Yet it often happens that the young people who thrive most during and after college are those who met with adversity early on, and gained awareness and maturity as a result of it.

Every child faces adversity in one form or another, from health problems to poverty, and from discrimination to family challenges. These experiences can be very painful, but if young people can learn from misfortune and grow, they not only set themselves up for great lives ahead, but they become inspirations to all whom they encounter, admissions officers included.

If your child has faced adversity in any way, first-hand or through a family or close friend, he or she can gain a profound sense of redemption, meaning, and purpose by transforming the experiences into positive action. They'll find that colleges practically fling open their doors to young people who can learn to celebrate their identity in this way.

As you read the stories that follow, notice how the students addressed the adversity in their lives, inspired those around them, and prepared themselves for the challenges of life ahead.

Kara from San Diego, California

Sparks: Passion for science, sensitivity, generosity
Inspiring Fire: Celebrating health

While we didn't work with Kara as a client, her story was too inspiring to pass up. Growing up, Kara watched her father and brother suffer from diabetes. After seeing loved ones suffer the ravages of the illness, she decided to dedicate herself to helping those with the disease. She excelled in biology classes her freshman year, and as a sophomore, her guidance counselors advised her to pursue further instruction at a local university program. That summer, she also worked at a hospital research lab and made time to visit with diabetes patients.

When she returned to school her junior year, she organized a diabetes-awareness group and a weeklong, school-wide forum to educate her peers on healthy eating habits and making healthy life choices. Her work garnered her recognition and entry into University of California, Berkeley with a full scholarship.

Discovered Brand: Student Leader, Public Health Activist

Bryce from Olympia, Washington

Sparks: Language talents, good with computers
Inspiring Fire: Celebrating cultural heritage

When we began working with Bryce, he told us his hope was to become a software engineer. His underlying ambition was to improve people's lives. As we got to know Bryce's family, we learned that his father was a member of the Cowlitz Tribe's General Counsel and the tribe was facing significant challenges. With declining numbers, the tribe's language was in danger of going extinct.

Bryce brainstormed ways he could help, and came up with a plan to digitize the language and store it online so that teachers, linguists, and members of the tribe could have ready access at any time. Bryce's language digitization project combined his personal talent with cultural pride. By his senior year, a number of prestigious schools had already begun actively soliciting Bryce to their campus.

Discovered Brand: Linguist, Computer Programmer

Antoine from Oakland, California

Sparks: Love of hip-hop, writing, courage
Inspiring Fire: Celebrating nonviolence

Though not a College Match client, Antoine has a story so inspiring we had to include it here. Antoine grew up in an Oakland neighborhood plagued by violence. By age twelve, he'd watched two of his closest friends get killed in neighborhood shootings. Through middle school, he himself had been in and out of trouble until he got admitted into a local outreach program called Upward Bound.

With their guidance, he became active in an after-school program that taught music production, especially socially-aware hip hop. During the summer and winter breaks, he attended anti-violence leadership conferences at a local university, and his junior year, he teamed up with other youth to write, direct, and produce an online TV series that brought a message of hope to inner-city youth across the country. Inspired to improve the plight of others in low-income areas, he gained admission to three prestigious colleges with vision and confidence in his future.

Discovered Brand: Media Producer

Wade from Kansas City, Missouri

Sparks: Love of computers, ingenuity, discipline
Inspiring Fire: Celebrating unique interests

Wade, 16, claimed to have no extracurricular activities. He didn't participate in any organized activities, sports, or clubs. He spent considerable time working on his computer, and had even learned to build a computer from scraps that he recycled from discarded computers. His other hobby involved carving and painting model figures of warriors that he'd invented himself. His ability to build computers and work diligently to create an elaborate fantasy world were impressive to us, but Wade had always thought his talents meaningless since he was relentlessly mocked and teased for his "weird" interests at school.

With our encouragement, he began taking pride in his creativity. He began inventing robots and listing his products online for sale. By his junior year, he'd started a business that was so profitable, he was able to hire several employees by the following summer. His "unpopular" interests were transformed into cool assets once he found the right community which prized his talents. The advancement of his talents and entrepreneurship won him admission to Willamette University.

Discovered Brand: Inventor

Exercise: Fire that inspires

(30 minutes)

Goal: To find ways to turn adversity into triumph.

Instructions:

1. Discuss ways your child has endured either adversity or the experience of being different. Try to look past the negative aspects of the experience and find ways that positive values of awareness, compassion, and strength can be developed.

2. Explore ways your child can learn to celebrate difference through action, service, and community-building. There might be programs that provide coaching and counseling that can help your child honor and celebrate being different.

7

HARNESSING FIRE:

scaling upwards

BUILDING VALUE TAKES time, usually a couple of years, so
if possible, we recommend getting started early in high school,
sophomore or even freshman year.

Once the fire of strong talents and interests gets lit, there's no reason to
stop. Building confidence and esteem to high levels assures that your
student will:

- Have a clear vision and purpose for the future to guide his
  college selection
- Convey her story with pride and excitement on her applications
- Head into college with strength and momentum

We have found in our work with young people that when they fuel
their sparks in their deepest ambitions, they consistently exceed their
wildest expectations. Potential has no limitations, and the discovery of
this fact is an integral part of the Brand U process that we call **Scaling**

Upwards. By Scaling Upwards, students take their skills and passions as far as they possibly can.

Scaling Upwards puts the defining touches on your child's accomplishments, allowing personal goals and achievements to build on themselves:

- If your student has completed a research project or won a competition or scholarship, these accomplishments can be used to raise awareness and bring a positive message through media recognition.
- If your student has created art or writing or has performed at a local level, that success can be used to build community support to push the accomplishments into state, national, and even international forums.
- If your student has started a business, nonprofit, club, or community program, that achievement can be expanded and replicated in locations beyond the local level.

scaling upwards: third-party recognition

In the ultra-competitive arena of college admissions, third-party recognition validates your student's ambition and purpose by profiling achievement in ways that colleges can see.

It's great if a student starts a nonprofit, but if that nonprofit gets written up in a newspaper or garners a positive quote from a mayor or civic leader, that achievement is suddenly awarded far more weight and importance. Likewise, if a young person forms an acting group that stages a play, that's great, but that achievement will be far greater if it's written up in the local paper.

Third-party recognition is a primary method for scaling upwards, and it's not as hard as it looks. With so many negative stories always swirling around, media outlets—from local papers and TV news to online media—are hungry for positive stories about young people taking initiative and making a difference.

Recognition can take any number of forms:

- Getting a research paper or journalistic piece published
- Getting profiled by TV news or newspaper for academic and extracurricular successes.
- Winning a science project, or getting one's name in the newspaper for starting a community service.
- Superlative comments from teachers for academic success
- Positive recognition from leadership figures

For college admissions, third-party recognition will make your student a "triple threat" in the eyes of admissions reps, taking the ambition and achievement and providing the substantiation they deserve. Remember, admissions officers only have fifteen minutes to learn who your student is. When colleges see that your student's hard work has been validated in this way, they'll fling their doors open.

I'm passionate about this point because it works every time. Third-party recognition ensures that your child's hard work stands out from the thousands of other applicants to make sure that their theme of value is clearly positioned in the minds of admission officers.

Sharon from Belmont, Massachusetts

Sparks: Love of computers, commitment, teamwork
Harnessing Fire: Third-party recognition

When we met Sharon as a sophomore, she spoke of her interests in computer science and engineering. Working with her parents, we explored ways that she could develop leadership skills in the field. During her sophomore year, she began pursuing opportunities through tech clubs and science fairs, and got involved in her school's Robotics Team. By her junior year, she'd earned the respect of her teammates and was chosen to lead the team. Dedicating herself to her passion, she coached her team in the invention of a brand new prototype robot, and earned a series of victories in science contests at the state, national, and ultimately international level.

Her achievement yielded her a story in a national magazine article celebrating youth in science, and her work garnered further recognition through a national "Women in the Sciences" award. She also earned a prestigious scholarship to attend USC.

Discovered Brand: Robotics Developer

We must note that some students will not feel comfortable pursuing third-party recognition for various reasons. Some don't enjoy being the center of the spotlight, and others may think that recognition is prideful. If your child feels this way, congratulate yourself on raising a sincere child.

At the same time, recognition is not about self-glorification. It's about building something much larger than oneself. Recognition can be used to raise awareness for worthy causes, unify the community, and inspire others to realize what is possible when a person takes action.

Exercise: Third-Party Recognition

(30 minutes)

Goal: To make sure your child's hard work and achievements get the validation they deserve.

Instructions:

1. Once your child has started developing in areas of leadership, service entrepreneurship, performance, art, writing, research, scholarships, or academic competition or scholarship, discuss ways that achievements can be used to:

    • Raise awareness for a worthy cause
    • Build community
    • Inspire or educate others

2. Explore avenues for achievements to get profiled, reviewed, or published through print, television, online media, or social media.

3. If your child gains recognition at the local level for good work, scale the recognition upwards to the state, regional, national, and even international level.

scaling upwards: balancing out a low grade

No one's perfect. All students has a place where they don't meet the highest standards. The bad news is that a weak spot in grades or test scores can significantly set your child back in the admissions process. The good news is that with a little focus and attention, potential deal-breakers can be improved or made up for.

In fact, the dedication and effort a student shows by overcoming weak spots in academics can actually inspire admissions boards to give a student added consideration.

Potential academic weaknesses include:

- Low GPA
- Low Test Scores
- Poor attendance

As admissions consultants, a big part of what we do is help students counterbalance the gaps in their performance. It's important to note, however, that **academic gaps cannot be filled by extracurricular per-formance.**

If grades are weak, extracurriculars won't help, whether it's volunteering or leadership, being an Eagle Scout or playing varsity sports. While those efforts are commendable, colleges need proof of strong academic commitment. They value academic performance first because they want to be certain that your child will not only survive, but thrive at their university.

At the same time, a few low grades don't have to ruin your child's college chances, and showing **excellence** in academic performance is the way forward. Here, Margaret did just that.

Margaret from Pasadena, California

Unique Sparks: Talented writer, imaginative, funny
Harnessing Fire: Balancing out low grades

Many students are creative, but some take creativity to new levels. When we began working with Margaret, she made it clear that she wanted to pursue creative writing at her dream school, Vassar College. The problem was that Margaret's GPA in math was several points lower than Vassar's cutoff GPA, and because she was already late in her junior year, there was little chance of retaking courses to raise her GPA.

We created a strategy, and with the help of College Match's writing specialist, Margaret compiled a scrapbook of poems, short stories, and humor pieces that she edited into a cohesive manuscript that she shared with her writing teachers and mentors who passed the manuscript along to other writers in the community, one of which happened to be a well-known novelist. This author loved the work and commented on it—praise that Margaret listed in her applications under Awards and Honors.

Next, we urged her to include an excerpt of her best writing, which had won her praise, in the Additional Information section of her Common Application, and finally, we had her send her manuscript to the head of Vassar's English Department. This did the trick! With positive support from within the faculty, Margaret was able to balance out her low math grades, and she was admitted Early Decision to Vassar.

Discovered Brand: Acclaimed Writer

PARENTS

Exercise: Balancing Out Low Grades

(30 minutes)

Goal: To strengthen any gaps in your student's academic record.

Instructions: For all classes where your student scored a B minus or lower, meet with teachers and find out about ways where he or she can improve or make up for low scores.

Order the book, What Smart Students Know, which offers valuable tips for making the grade, and go through it with your student.

Next, decide on ways to balance out low grades:

- Summer school
- Private tutoring school
- University bridge program
- Academic research project
- Publishing

Make a plan with your student to strengthen any gaps. Consult teachers and guidance counselors as needed.

Exercise: Scaling Upwards

(30 minutes)

Goal: To help your child build on previous achievements.

Instructions:

1. See that your student begins keeping a master list of his or her experiences and achievements starting at the end of 8th grade.

2. Look for ways to keep building your student's passion and skill. If he has success at the school level, see if he can take it to the community level. If she has started a community organization, see if she can replicate it at a regional or even national level. Keep the fire going.

3. Explore ways that your student can raise awareness and get media attention to create community and momentum for his projects. Media awareness can also help causes your student cares about.

fire: parting thoughts

As we prepare to move on, we take stock in all the achievements your student has made thus far, the hard work of embracing one's uniqueness and pursuing one's path. These efforts will prove vital as we move forward into the second half of the book, through the work of college selection and college admissions.

In Part III, the fire your child has lit will provide the vision and enlightenment to see the future that feels best and to find the right undergraduate experience to achieve that future.

BRAND U

Fire

- We ignite the sparks of your child's unique talents and interests through developing transformative paths of leadership, service, creativity, and entrepreneurship.

- The **deep ambitions** underneath your child's hopes and dreams will fuel growth of transformative experiences.

- There are many different unique experiences to ignite your child's talents, passions, and ambitions, among which are **university programs, unique employment, research, scholarships and academic competitions, performance, and portfolio creation.**

- Incredible value can be found in **celebrating unique difference** and **overcoming adversity**, transformative efforts that reflect maturity and courage and ensure integrity in the challenges of life ahead.

- Build the power of past accomplishments by using the fire of motivation to **scale upwards**, gain **third-party recognition**, and **shore up gaps** in your child's academic record.

- **Welcome mistakes and setbacks** as learning experiences, and don't worry about failure or embarrassment.

- **Take small, incremental steps** to avoid feeling overwhelmed.

- **Seek help from mentors and admissions consultants** if the process becomes too challenging.

PART III

Sparks
Fire
VISION
Brand

COLLEGE SELECTION BEGINS with Vision.

At College Match, we consider choosing a college as the **first adult decision** in a young person's life.

Unfortunately, too many students approach this life-altering choice in an *adolescent* way, which doesn't make for a happy and fulfilled adulthood. Choosing the right college isn't easy, nor should it be. The most meaningful elements in life seldom are easy.

The good news is that everything we have done so far has prepared your student for the selection process. With the tools of self-discovery gained thus far, students will be able to:

- Envision the life they want to have during and after college
- Find the undergraduate experience to fulfill their hopes and goals
- Pinpoint the exact schools that fit their values and personality

College selection is an exciting time, fueled with hope and possibility. We want your child to look back on this time with gratitude for a decision about their future life made with care.

TYPICAL PARENT TRAPS

"Harvard and Yale guarantee success in life, right?"

"I know the best place for my kid."

"My kid's college is a reflection of my parenting."

"Ivy League graduates have better lives."

"How exactly do we choose?"

CLEAR VISION:

selection 101

CHOOSING A COLLEGE is a momentous decision and can feel overwhelming to parents and students alike. The challenge of trying to choose from hundreds of different schools is one reason that so many young people default to an easier route.

Too often, the selection process is done in a haphazard, random way based on favorite football teams, magazine rankings, name recognition, and social life. As a result, only 60% of students finish in four years and about a third transfer out of their college and/ or department before graduation, at enormous financial cost and frustration.

The Brand U method is designed to help young people avoid the mistakes that cause thousands of students each year to deeply regret their college choice.

selection 101: the homebuyer analogy

Tuition costs have doubled in the last ten years. Private and out-of-state public universities now add up to $200,000 for four years, and in-state public schools top $80,000. Next to buying a home, a college education is the most expensive investment a family can make.

Who would dare buy a house based simply on word of mouth, without ever getting to know the floor plan and inspecting everything from the plumbing and wiring to the vibe of the surrounding area? Who would spend that amount of money without carefully checking the specs and hiring a contractor to make sure the house was both sound and the right fit for their family?

Consider the consequences beyond financial costs for choosing the wrong house: frustration, resentment, dashed expectations, unhappiness with location, regret for not choosing more wisely. And yet these are the very same emotions that thousands of young people experience each year when they transfer, drop out, or simply find themselves unengaged at the college they selected.

If your son or daughter chooses by superficial standards and if things go wrong, the disappointment and frustration will live with them for many years.

selection 101: pitfalls

Before we explore **how to choose**, we'll take a moment to discuss **how *not* to choose**, particularly the three major pitfalls of college selection, as well as the **superficial standards** by which well-intentioned parents and kids get misguided.

pitfall #1: prestige frenzy

Prestige is paramount to many parents, understandably so. Elite schools carry the aura of success, the sense that everything that follows for the child will turn out rosy, and that the parent can sit back and bask in having done everything right.

In our culture, there's no higher merit badge of parental excellence than having a child at one of the nation's "elite" schools. I'm often presented with this fact in my work with clients, and to you I'll pose the question I always pose to them:

Which is better, the *best* school or the *right* school?

As someone who has spent nearly two decades in the industry, I assure you, prestige does not equal success, and prestige definitely does not equal happiness. What creates long-term success and happiness is when students find the undergraduate experience that best fits their unique values, purpose, and vision for life.

Next to this grounded and authentic approach, chasing prestige turns out to be just another superficial siren. Part of the problem is the perception that one can only get the "best" education and connections at the Ivies, MIT or Stanford. These schools do good business selling the idea that they somehow hold the golden ticket to happiness and success.

Yet, roughly 90 percent of Fortune 500 CEO's didn't need an Ivy League education to maximize their potential. And, with less than 1% of college graduates attending an Ivy, it's difficult to make the case that everyone who didn't attend an Ivy League college is either unhappy or unsuccessful. If you look closer at the numbers, you quickly realize that an Ivy League education is a fantasy that 99% of us do not achieve in reality. Remember, college is not the destination, it's your life. You don't want people saying when you die that the best thing that you did was attend a particular college.

pitfall #2: choosing by magazine rankings

The yearly magazine rankings are major culprits of the prestige myth. One of the biggest mistakes students make is choosing their future by numerical rankings. While rankings might be useful in sports, which are based on contests with clear winners and losers, college rankings are based on a random collection of questionable standards that shed no light on whether an undergraduate experience is the right fit for a young person.

Yet, each year, those rankings trick parents and students into using inverted logic, that to get into the "best" school possible means applying to #1, and if that doesn't work, #5, then #12, or as "good" as we can get. Or maybe we try for the "best" school in our region or the "best" school with a great football team and a fun party reputation.

Realize, first of all, that these rankings are highly subjective, or fluffy, and that it's not a good idea to build your child's future on something *fluffy*. You want strong data and hard facts.

Secondly the "experts" who rank these universities know nothing about your child's unique strengths, passions, or life vision, the elements which should be the defining metrics of the school your student chooses to attend.

Lastly, you want your student to be at a school that is dedicated to its students. Loren Pope, the famed admission consultant, proved as much. In his groundbreaking book, *Looking Beyond the Ivy League,* he shows how smaller liberal arts colleges outperform their Ivy league counterparts in major skill sets, including academics, social networking, social life, and even job placement.

Status is attractive, but college is a long-term relationship. Do you want your child to base such a life-altering choice on something so superficial?

pitfall #3: deciding for your kid

Many parents want to play a starring role in what should be a young person's biggest act. With the stakes so high, it can be tempting for parents to want to jump in and help direct the show. While this is an understandable impulse, the consequences of intervening in your child's first adult decision are great and costly.

Parents, unless you're planning to move into your child's dorm and watch over his every move, we advise that you entrust the responsibility of choosing to your student. How can a young person feel fully invested if he doesn't make the choice of college for herself and if he isn't given the trust to chart her own destiny? In effect, choosing a school for your child is tantamount to keeping your child...a child.

Once in college, students have to be self-motivated and fully invested in the school they've chosen.

selection 101: vision is power

We turn now from the pitfalls you'll want to avoid and move towards the glorious potential your child can seek. The good news is that choosing the right college is not only manageable, but the collaboration in doing so is richly rewarding, allowing you to support and strengthen your child in this momentous time.

In the sections to come, we'll lay out steps to prepare you and your student for the challenges ahead. Going forward, we'll match your student's values and vision for the future with the colleges that'll make that vision a reality.

Right now, we begin by exploring the vision your child has for the future. Your hopes and wishes play an important part here. Be sure to share them, but also be sure to let your student elucidate the vision born of his or her own unique fire.

We find that what most surprises parents is how mature their teenagers turn out to be when given the tools to create their own future. We begin building that future now.

Exercise: Your Future College Grad #1

(30 minutes)

Goal: To help you envision what you want the college experience to mean to your child.

Instruction: Write freely on all possible hopes you have for your child's future. What kind of life do you want your child to have upon graduation? What do you hope he will have gained and experienced from his time in college? Think about your big hopes, like happiness, fulfillment, and confidence. What do they look like for your child?

Exercise: Your Future College Grad #1

(30 minutes)

Goal: To help your child express what they want out of life.

Instruction: Follow the steps below.

Get out of the house, and go somewhere fun, perhaps outdoors and definitely with a relaxed state of mind. When you've settled into a good spot, let your child talk at length about the following questions. The point is not to argue about what's wrong or right, but to help your child conduct a college search in a heartfelt and mature way. Foster the exploration process without being directive.

- How do you want to develop in college? What do you want your life to look like after college? Given your favorite experiences thus far, what would be your top dream jobs?

- What skills and passions do you want to develop in college? What are some majors and extracurriculars that will prepare you for the life you want to have after college?

- What education will be necessary? Will grad school be necessary, or will you need to be prepared for your dream career right out of college?

ENLIGHTENED VISION:

undergraduate types

BRAND U BEGINS with students' visions of the life they want to live and how they need to develop to realize their hopes for life. Once these visions are identified, we explore which type of undergraduate experience will take each student where he or she wants to go in life.

Unlike magazine rankings, which use highly simplistic descriptions like *National, Doctoral, Research, Regional,* we group colleges and universities by the life preparation they offer and which students they best serve. Accordingly, we break undergraduate schools into seven different types:

Specialty Schools

- Research Universities
- Polytechnics/Land Grant Universities
- Liberal Arts Colleges
- Hybrid Universities
- Teaching Colleges/Comprehensives

Descriptions follow for each type. With your student, take some time to get acquainted with the strengths and weaknesses of the types of universities and the kind of students each school is geared toward. As you go, discuss which type of school feels like the best match for fulfilling the needs, intentions, and hopes your child has for the future.

Specialty Schools

Recommended to:
Students who wish to be career-ready right out of college in the fields of engineering, business, technology, science, design, or the performing arts, and seek training in a highly competitive environment before entering the workforce.

Size
Small—between 500 and 3,000 students.

Description
Specialty schools offer intensive professional preparation in a particular field. Students build portfolios of training experience to offer future employers upon graduation. That said, specialty schools tend to be weak in humanities and social sciences since they focus on one particular field.

Strengths
Excellent job prospects at competitive salaries upon graduation. Strong graduate school placement.

Weaknesses
Lack of well-rounded education.

Specialty Schools by Field
- **Art & Design:** Pratt, RISD, SCAD, North Carolina School of the Arts, Cornish College of the Arts, Cooper Union
- **Performance:** Berkelee, Juilliard
- **Engineering:** Harvey Mudd, Olin, Cooper Union
- **Business:** Babson

Research Universities

Recommended to:
Extroverted and assertive students who won't get lost in the crowd or let large class sizes detract from their educational experience.

Size
Large (10,000) to very large (up to 40,000)

Description
Research Universities are so-named for *doctorate* level research for industries such as defense, technology and pharmaceuticals. So far as undergraduates are concerned, these schools offer famous names and athletic programs, and a variety of majors. **However, classes tend to be held in lecture halls, or are taught by graduate students instead of professors. Due to their size, students at these schools get less personalized attention or mentorship than they would at smaller schools.**

Strengths
Graduating students get recruited by various industries, and assertive students can take advantage of numerous job networking opportunities on campus.

Shortcomings
Less effective at graduate school preparation than liberal arts colleges. Unless you're highly assertive, Research U's offer less personal development, which means your potential doesn't get maximized, and you finish college less prepared than you might otherwise be at a smaller school.

Examples of Research Universities
University of California, Michigan,Wisconsin, Berkeley, Illinois, UNC, Washington, Maryland, Brown, Columbia, Cornell, Dartmouth, Harvard, Penn, Princeton, Yale, Vanderbilt, Duke, Northwestern, Tulane, Stanford, USC, UMass, BU, John Hopkins, University of Chicago.

Polytechnic/Land Grant Universities

Recommended to:
Students who want job preparation in engineering, technology, business, architecture, and agriculture, and who seek a larger learning environment with more course offerings than specialty schools offer.

Size
Large, 10,000 or more undergraduates.

Description
Polytechnics were developed using agriculture and engineering land grants for agriculture. (They often have cows on campus.) Nowadays, they focus on many practical and theoretical fields (hence, *'poly-technic'*) in a variety of courses and majors.

Strengths
Strong professional development in specific programs. While these are usually less competitive at career training than specialty schools, you get more academic variety and an active campus life.

Shortcomings
Polytechnics don't tend to be as strong in grad school placement as liberal arts or small research universities.

Examples of Polytechnics/ Land Grant Colleges
CalPoly, Auburn, Ohio State U, Colorado State U, Oregon State U, Washington State U, Penn State U, Cornell U, UC Davis, Arizona Polytech at Arizona State U, NY Poly, Michigan State, Virginia Polytechnic, Texas A&M, RPI.

Liberal Arts Colleges

Recommended to:
All students who wish to attend grad school. Liberal arts colleges have the best track record for grad school placement and outperform larger research universities in prestigious scholarships like the Fulbright and Rhodes.

Size
Small campuses with student bodies between 500 and 2000.

Description
Liberal arts colleges are small and personalized campuses where students engage closely with faculty and are pushed to express themselves and think critically in a large variety of majors. Class sizes are small and students receive excellent personal attention and mentorship from professors, with opportunities to perform research coauthored by professors.

Strengths
Liberal Arts colleges do an outstanding job of preparing students for elite graduate schools in law, business, and medicine, as well as PhD programs. Many liberal arts colleges have 3:2 joint-programs with Ivy League graduate schools.

Shortcomings
More focused on grad school preparation, Liberal Arts colleges are less geared towards preparing students for careers right out of college. Graduates perform very well, however, in pay scale rankings ten years after college.

Examples of Liberal Arts Colleges
Amherst, Swarthmore, Claremont McKenna, Kenyon, Occidental, Beloit, Hamilton, Grinnell, Amherst, Williams, Wesleyan, Bennington, Whittier, Puget Sound, Whitman, Willamette U, Evergreen State College.

Hybrid Universities

Recommended to:
Students who want to hedge the experience of a research university and a liberal arts college.

Size
Typically between 2500—6000 undergraduate.

Description
Hybrids straddle the ground between research universities and liberal arts colleges. They provide some research at the graduate level and some focus on writing, critical thinking and public speaking. The Catholic Loyola's are perfect examples. Smaller research universities that offer higher professor interaction qualify for this category.

Strengths
Hybrids tend to have better job placement than Liberal Arts, by offering strong regional job networks. Hybrids also afford students more personal attention from professors than is possible at large research universities.

Shortcoming
Hybrids don't perform as well as the Liberal Arts in getting students into grad school, though elite hybrids are an exception to this rule.

Examples of Hybrids
Santa Clara, Seattle University, University of Denver, University of Redlands, Loyola Marymount University, Villanova University, Elon University, James Madison University, Creighton, Gonzaga, Chapman University, University of Portland, Pacific Lutheran, Regis University, Fairfield University, Bentley University, Ithaca College, Alfred University, University of Dallas

Teaching College/Comprehensives

Recommended to:
Students seeking credentialing programs for jobs, such as teaching K-12 in a specific state.

Size
4,000 to 20,000 undergraduate.

Description
These colleges were originally set up to educate pre-K-12 teachers. In recent decades, many teachers colleges have added other fields of study, becoming comprehensive in their offerings. A good example is Arizona State which now offers a communications school, business program, science and engineering campus and a well-regarded honors college.

Strengths
Comprehensives offer good credentialing programs and usually afford students with personalized attention from professors and smaller class sizes.

Shortcomings
Credentials offered by these schools often do not cross state lines. These programs tend to emphasize formulaic coursework, with little room for questioning, challenging, or critical analysis of accepted methods.

Examples of Teachers Colleges/ Comprehensives
Arizona State U, All California State Universities (Chico, California State University San Francisco State U, San Diego State U, Central Washington U, Western Washington U, Southern Illinois U, Bowling Green, Kent State, Sam Houston State, San Jose State, Western Oregon State University

Tips for Choosing Undergraduate Type

Based on your child's life vision, explore which type of school fits best.

- If your child has a singular focus on becoming an engineer, science, art, or performing arts, and wishes to pursue a career out of college which will require a highly advanced level of training, then look at **Specialty Schools**.

- If your child wishes to pursue agriculture, engineering, business, and architecture right out of college but wants a larger campus with more variety than a specialty school can offer, look at the **Polytechnics**.

- If your child is extroverted, assertive, and focused enough that a very large institution will enhance rather than reduce growth, then look at **Research Universities**.

- If your child wants an excellent, well-rounded education, strong personal development, and entrance into grad school after college, refine search to **Liberal Arts Colleges**.

- If your child wants the variety of a research university at a smaller sized school, then refine search to **Hybrid Universities**.

- If your child wishes to get credentialed as a K-12 teacher within a particular region, then refine search to **Teaching College/ Comprehensives**.

Exercise: Your Child's Undergraduate Type

(30 minutes)

Goal: To help your child choose the optimal type.

Instructions: Follow the steps below.

1. Does your child's dream career require graduate school or being career ready right out of college?

   Choose One: ☐ **Grad School**   ☐ **Career Ready**

2. If your child's vision includes graduate school, think:

   • Liberal Arts Colleges
   • Small (Private) Research Universities

   If that vision involves being career-ready out of undergrad, choose from one of the following based on your child's field of development:

   • Specialty Schools
   • Polytechnics
   • Large (Public) Research Universities
   • Hybrids
   • Teaching Colleges/Comprehensives

3. Based on your answers to the previous questions, choose the undergraduate type that will best fulfill your child's hopes and goals.

   Optimal Undergraduate Type -

Think Like An Admissions Officer
College Selection

As an admissions officer, you've been entrusted by your university to determine which applicants will fit your school and which won't. Each application has a supplemental essay, where students express why they want to attend your particular university.

It's hard to believe, but most of the applications you get are from kids who have no idea what kind of school they're applying to. You can tell immediately which students picked you from your prestige, ranking, football program, or some other superficial reason because those students always give clichés and generalizations about how wonderful your school is and how excited they'd be to receive admission. If you had a nickel for every time a student used shameless flattery to get into your school, you could retire tomorrow.

But every so often, you read an essay from a student who's different, someone who has actually invested time into the research process. You read his essay and he accurately describes the strengths of your program. He knows about your campus culture and about where students are satisfied. (He even knows where students aren't satisfied!)

His knowledge and preparation testify to both his investment in your school and to his high level of maturity, exactly the kind of student you want to have on your campus.

Now, if you had to choose between the highly-invested student and the cliché student, which would you say is better-suited to thrive on your campus and maximize his potential?

"What kind of financial aid does each school offer?"

"Are classes taught by professors or teaching assistants?"

"Do any of the programs offer paid, on-the-job training?"

"What salaries do graduates earn right out of college?"

"How successful is each college in graduate school placement?"

"Are class sizes small enough for personal interaction with professors?"

10

FOCUSING VISION:

selection standards

FIRST, WE BRUSHED aside selection pitfalls like the party scene, football teams, and magazine rankings. Then, we defined the undergraduate type that will best serve your student's future. Now, we explore specific programs within the right undergraduate type to pinpoint the individual schools that fit your student's needs.

From our years of experience at College Match, we've found that there are **four standards** you want to use when choosing the right school. These are the elements that foretell the experiences students will have in college, from the moment they arrive on campus until they are sitting in interviews for post-graduate jobs or grad school.

The four standards we use to find the right fit for your student are:

- Real World Preparation
- Student Satisfaction
- Campus Culture
- Tuition and Financial Aid

For each of these standards, we offer metrics: specific ways of measuring and determining the schools that deliver the greatest value where your student needs it most. These metrics gauge everything from pay scale for graduates, to classroom environment, to the types and amounts of financial aid a school offers.

Information is readily accessible online and in any up-to-date college prospectus. You can also consult your student's guidance counselor to find up-to-date information.

While the legwork may seem daunting at first, don't let that hold your child back. Once students get going, the research gets easier as young people get a better picture of what they're looking for and what they want. Whatever inertia may be there at first will be cleared away once students get excited about their personal investment in their future.

Conducting Research on Colleges

1) College Review Sites

Knowing what the college has to say about itself versus what others have to say about it—online, in print and elsewhere—is a great way to compare and contrast to find shortcomings. For example, you might read comments from students at each college on StudentsReview.com and CollegeConfidential.com

2) Interview Current Students and Administrators

There's nothing like on-the-ground information. Often, these people know the most about areas where a college needs development. Interviews can give you insight as to where your student's strengths could be most valuable to the school.

3) University Websites

Get to know the college's website, its staff, its programs, and offerings. The typical university website can be daunting at first, but stick around, visit it a few nights in a row, and you'll start reading "between the lines" to see their soft spots, the areas they're hoping to improve, and the image they're trying to present.

4) College Prospectus Books

New editions are published each year. Often they'll have sections on each school, indicating where the school has shortcomings or low ratings. Examples include, The Insider's Guide to the Colleges, Fiske Guide to the Colleges and the website CollegeData.com.

"Real World" Preparation

Graduate School Placement
Use this metric if grad school is likely in your plans. Schools are rated by the percentage of seniors who earn enrollment into masters, PhD, and professional schools (law, business, and medicine).

Pay Scale *Upon* Graduation
College is an investment in your future. How do the colleges you're looking at rate against one another in the career fields you're interested in?

Pay Scale *Ten Years After* Graduation
This metric offers you an idea of long-term earning potential, and takes into account the benefits of attending graduate school. Often Liberal Arts schools have lower pay scales at graduation, but rank among the highest ten years after graduation.

Reputation in Chosen Field
Explore how strong a particular program is at each school in the areas of expertise that your child wishes to develop for the future.

Study/Internship Programs for Credit
This can be an excellent way for students to learn on the job, gain experience and career development, and build important connections before entering the real world.

Student Satisfaction

Average class size

Small classes mean an engaging classes taught professors versus classes fielded by TAs in large lecture hall or auditoriums. Class size can mean the difference between flourishing through personal relationships or losing focus from the lack thereof. Class size is also a big sign as to how much a college cares about their students' experience, whether they see their undergrads as individuals or numbers. (Note: Some larger private schools hire more professors in order to keep their class sizes smaller.)

Percentage of students who graduate within 4 or 5 years

This important figure reveals how successful a college is in helping its students stay focused on their academic goals. A high percentage of students graduating within 4 or 5 years is a good sign. Beware of schools with lower rates of students graduating on time.

Percentage of freshman who transfer

This figure is an excellent indicator of how happy or unhappy students are at any given college. A significant number of freshmen transfer or simply drop out of college after their first year. Right now, about one third of US college students transfer. Checking the numbers on freshman retention can help you avoid an unhappy experience from the beginning.

Best orientation and first-year transition programs

This determines how a school treats its incoming freshman. The first impression of a school goes a long way to shape a student's educational experience.

Poll current students and recent graduates

Current students and recent grads can provide excellent real-time information on the collegiate experience at a university.

Campus Culture

Institutional mission
Mission statements tell a lot about a college's values. Also read about the original founding and intent. (Wikipedia is a great source for this information.)

Public vs. private
Public schools often have a very different dynamic than private schools. Weigh the trade-offs of both and decide which feels best.

Location
You may want to be in the middle of an urban center or in a small town with only nature for miles. Another consideration is whether the school is located near an economic hub for your particular field, which is often the case in fields such as technology, agriculture, and the performing arts.

Breakdown of student body by majors
What majors are students specializing in? How many departments does the college have, and which departments have they been recognized for? Which departments receive the most funding? How do these answers align with what you want to get out of college?

Diversity on Campus
What is the ethnic, social, and class diversity on campus? How homogenous is the climate in terms of nationality and religion? Is the student body known for being open or close-minded? Does the campus have a reputation for being traditional and conservative, liberal and outspoken, or somewhere in between?

Tuition & Financial Aid

Tuition
Consider the cost of living along with tuition, as certain locations are far more expensive than others. *In-state* public universities are typically less expensive while *out-of-state* publics tend to cost as much as private schools. Private schools often make up for the price difference by offering generous financial aid packages.

Types of Financial Aid Offered
With the already-high price of undergraduate education rising each year, debt is a major concern. You should take financial aid into account for every school you consider. Most colleges offer both need-based and merit-based financial aid. Look for schools that are known for their generosity in this regard.

Merit Aid
At College Match, we pride ourselves on securing merit aid for the majority of our students. 96% of our clients were accepted into the college of their dreams and 92% of our clients won merit scholarships averaging $57,250.

One place to learn how schools stack up is Kiplinger's "100 Best Value Schools," an annual issue including such factors as spending per student, merit-based awards, and financial aid. You can find the latest survey here: http://www.kiplinger.com/tools/colleges/.

Exercise: What are your Mandatories?

(1 hour)

Goal: To compare prospective schools side by side.

Instructions:

1. Make a table like the one below. Place college names at the top.

2. On the left, list the standards that you care about. Use the Internet or college prospectus to find how your schools compare.

Metrics	Colleges				
	College 1	College 2	College 3	College 4	College 5
Tuition					
Ratio of Professors to Students					
Percent Graduating in 4 or 5 years					
Class Size					
Insert Standard					

Exercise: Create an "I" List

(30 minutes)

Goal: To help clarify the schools your child likes best.

Instructions:

1. After comparing the qualities of different schools, it's good to make a list of at least nine or ten that your child feels good about.

2. For each prospective school, encourage your child to make an "I" list to express what he or she likes best about the school in terms of real world experience, campus experience, student satisfaction, and affordability. Try to list as many positive reasons as possible.

   For example :

   - I like the campus.
   - I like the location.
   - I high student satisfaction rate.
   - I like the generous Merit scholarships...

3. Go over the "I list" together, and discuss which schools feel like the best fit, comparing the ways each school can what your child seeks from an undergraduate experience. Weigh the options together, and let your child determine the schools that **feel** best.

Beware of Blinders

Making the first adult decision in one's life isn't easy. Here are some of the selection pitfalls to watch out for:

blinder #1: superficials
If your student is caught by the lure of party reputation, athletics, or other superficial aspects of a school, help him think about the trade-offs in the long run.

blinder #2: impatience
College research takes time and effort, but it's not too hard if organized into manageable "bites." By breaking up the work to just one hour a week starting their junior year, students can establish a strong idea of where they want to go when its time to apply their senior year.

blinder #3: feeling overwhelmed
If all else fails, take heart in knowing that admissions consultants like College Match are available to help you at every stage of the game. With years of experience and tools for insight, we can help your student thrive through the challenges of selection and admission.

11

PROPER VISION:
the right match

HOPEFULLY, YOUR STUDENT has begun finding schools that inspire **excitement** about the future, and you as parents are excited too, seeing how your child's passions and talents will burn brighter on those campuses.

We're almost to the end, with just a little further to go. The next steps of the method will help build confidence in the selections your student has made. Finding the right match involves:

- Tiering schools by admission chances
- Interviewing current students at prospective schools
- Visiting prospective campuses

the right match: tier by admission chances
We recommend selecting at least nine schools to apply to. It's important for students to have fallback schools. While more schools means more effort, it also means more options, and more doors of

opportunity to match your student's vision and personality. It takes a little extra effort, but that extra effort pays off for a lifetime.

Once your student has a collection of schools together, we want to tier those schools by the likelihood of getting admittance. We want to make sure that:

1. Your student has fallbacks
2. Your student is excited about those fallbacks

We like to see at least two or three schools represented in each of the following tiers:

- **Super-reach schools** (less than 10% chance of getting in)
- **Reach schools** (10-25%)
- **Fifty-fifty schools** (50%)
- **Safety schools** (>75%+)

These tiers are determined by schools' selectivity ratings and each student's performance and tiers are different for each student.

Guidance counselors and professional consultants can give you quick and helpful assessments to figure out how different schools stack up. Keep in mind, students who seek merit aid should weight their schools more heavily to the lower tiers. Remember that less prestigious schools pay more to get strong students than highly prestigious schools, which have thousands of strong students applying to them already.

Exercise: Tiering By Admission

(30 minutes)

Goal: To ensure your child has schools in each tier.

Instructions: With the help of a guidance counselor or professional consultant, help your child organize prospective schools into tiers of super-reach, reach, fifty-fifty, and safety schools. Doing this early on will help to ensure that your child feels good about all the options.

the right match: student interviews

Current students are the best source for accurate, up-to-date information about their universities. By interviewing them, your student will be able to find the right school and avoid ending up at the wrong one. We recommend that our clients interview several students at each school, particularly in one's field of study.

Some young people shy away from the idea of interviews for one reason or another, often out of not wanting to "bother" college students. If this is the case, parents can help them get over this hump by sharing the following facts:

- College students **love** sharing their opinions and advice
- While intimidating at first, **interviews are actually a lot of fun**
- Students can offer a **more honest perspective** than admission office representatives and campus tour leaders

Each interview will offer a host of unique opinions, so it's important to interview several students to avoid getting influenced by an outlier. Your student wants to look for recurring themes, positives, or negatives that keep popping up. Students at one school might feel that their professors are really engaged and supportive (awesome!) or students at another school might be so dissatisfied they're protesting the way the administration treats them. Again, this is all vitally important information!

After the interviews, discuss with your student in what ways the new information changes things. Does it make her want to fill out an application or run the other way? Either way, interviews empower your child to feel invested in the college selection process.

Exercise: Student Interviews

(30 minutes)

Goal: To make a wise college choice.

Instructions: There's no better way to know what your child is getting from a college than to **interview students** at prospective schools. Admissions offices will happily provide contacts of students that your child can interview. Try to interview students who have the same major that your child wishes to pursue.

the right match: campus visits

Once students have narrowed down the schools to the select few, you want them to get real-time experience at the school to make sure they can see themselves spending four years there. The worst thing students can do is apply blindly and then arrive on campus to a rude awakening.

University programs, usually offered during the summer and winter breaks, are a great way for students to get an extended on-campus experience. As for traditional college visits, we recommend that families visit during the spring break of high school junior year, so that you can see how the campuses feel **while students are present**. In the summertime, the colleges are nearly empty and lack the vibe your student will get during the school year.

To make the most of any campus visit, you also want to plan ahead so that your student can:

- Tour classrooms, dorms, cafeterias, and lab facilities
- Get an overnight stay on or near campus
- Interview the department chair for relevant majors
- Conduct on-the-spot interviews with five to ten students

Exercise: Campus Visits

(30 minutes)

Goal: To instill confidence in your child's selections.

Instructions: Plan ahead by calling or emailing school admissions offices to set up appointments and interviews with deans of admission, department chairs, and current students.

the right match: parting thoughts

The journey of selecting which colleges to apply to is nearly complete. I encourage all of my students to do some serious soul-searching before making their final decision about which colleges to choose. When students work through the steps previously mentioned, they're more than prepared to make the first adult decision of their lives.

The more deeply invested students feel about their choice of schools, the more they convey excitement and passion, the key qualities admissions officers look for in the application process. Make that investment now, and your child will look back on this moment with pride for decades to come.

BRAND U

Vision Review

- Be careful to **avoid the pitfalls** of **prestige frenzy, college rankings,** and choosing colleges based on convenience factors such as cost and/or location or familiarity.

- Start the selection process with a vision of **your child's hopes and goals**. Then explore the educational needs that will make your child's vision a reality.

- Find the **type of undergraduate experience** that will help your child develop into the person he or she wants to become.

- Narrow the focus on individual schools by comparing measurements like **real-world preparation, student support services, campus culture,** and **financial aid.** The **"I" List** can help your child clarify which schools feel best.

- Once your child has a group of favorite choices, be sure to **tier schools by admission,** and then **conduct interviews** and **college visits** to shore up confidence in the selections.

- If at any time you feel lost, confused, or overwhelmed, admissions consultants like College Match can restore confidence in the process.

PART IV

Sparks
Fire
Vision
BRAND

FOR NEARLY TWO decades, the Montesano Method has helped students get admitted to their first-choice colleges. The key element of the method is the Brand, the tool for which this book is named, a tool that empowers students. The Brand allows students to convey the fire of their vision and purpose through an ironclad statement of identity.

Too many students, not knowing any better, fill out their applications without a strategy and send them in, hoping for the best, not realizing just how extraordinarily competitive admissions has become. In many cases, applying to highly-selective schools is no better than playing the lottery.

This section will guide you in helping your student craft and sharpen a Brand that establishes your child's proven talents and passions. It will also help your student add value to schools in ways that no other applicant can.

12

CRAFTING THE BRAND:

unique value

MOST STUDENTS JUST fill out the application and send it in, never imagining that someone on the other end is getting thousands of applications with great grades and strong extracurricular activities. Savvy admission officers quickly notice who has taken the time to craft a unified theme and who hasn't. A cohesive message is a mark of maturity that exemplifies value, which is why the value a student brings to a college is so critical to the application process.

Earlier we talked about how when admissions officers read your application, it plays out like a movie of whom you are. Nothing helps convince admissions boards like a clear and concise vision that distills your student's talents and vision down to two or three unique facets that resonate through all of his or her accomplishments.

So how *do* you stand out against the competition?

The way you stand out happens to be that one core thing we've been working on from the beginning of your journey: **uniqueness.** The way you convey uniqueness is through the Brand statement, a message of unique value, which answers **the four main questions colleges want to know:**

- Who is the student?
- What makes him or her special?
- What value does he offer our school?
- Will her presence fill a gap at our university?

unique value: compile a Master List

A college application is a pretty static thing. Look at any of them and you'll see the same basic sections—educational data, test information, academic honors, and extracurricular activities—with the same basic blanks, lines, boxes, and squares allotted for each one.

When your student applies to college, the admissions reps will read the application quickly, with a laser focus for clues. Your student will have ten to fifteen minutes to make an impression on these four key questions. A college application offers only a small space for students to make their mark, so every element has to count. Each activity, hobby, club, honor, and achievement has to elucidate your student's sense of purpose.

Exercise: The Master List

(30 minutes)

Goal: To create a Master List to use for the application process.

Instructions:

1. Take out a clean sheet of paper. With your child, list all activities, jobs, clubs, sports, accomplishments, and recognitions.

2. Discuss which achievements and experiences best convey your child's unique value, the ones your child will want to highlight as representative of who he or she is.

unique value: make the *Muv*

Savvy admissions officers quickly judge an application by who has—*and who doesn't have*—a unified theme, the mark of maturity and purpose that gets your child admitted.

The *Muv* (Message of Unique Value) Statement is the application's theme, the heart and soul that unifies all of the grades, scores, and extracurriculars into one meaningful statement of a student's overarching ambition in life.

A college application affords only a small space for students to make their mark, so everything that gets put down has to be tied to this one compelling message. The following examples are taken from past clients, students whose strong *Muv* Statements propelled them to admissions success. As you read through, notice how each one harnesses the fire of academic and extracurricular excitement into a compelling message of unique value.

Martin Barlow—Uniquely Daring

Accomplishments
State Bike Racing Champion
3.5 GPA academic achievement
Published article in local paper, "How Racing Made Me a Better Student."
Member of Volunteer Medical Assistance Team in Haiti

Muv Statement:
"Martin Barlow brings the same daring and talent that makes him an award-winning cyclist to his academic studies and volunteer work, taking bold risks to make the world a better place."

Chad Phipps—Uniquely Able

Accomplishments
3.78 GPA
Won his division at the county science fair
Started a club for fellow wheelchair-bound students
Was featured on the local news

Muv Statement:
"Chad Phipps hasn't let the fact that he's wheelchair-bound slow him down one bit, dedicating himself to academics and scientific achievement and helping fellow students with disabilities get the most out of life."

Jessica Stemmler — Unique Excellence

Accomplishments from beginning of 9th grade to present:

4.0 GPA

Lead Trainer at local Stables

Three-time 4H Competition Champion

Summer study, Large Animal Medicine, UC Davis

Muv Statement:

"Jessica's standard of excellence has made her a top student, champion rider, and skilled trainer, motivating her to apply her talents and experience through serving in the field of large animal medicine."

While you haven't met these kids, their Muv Statements offer a vibrant picture of their talents and ambitions, an incredible asset that empowered these students to their top-choice schools.

Timing is essential here. It's critical to craft this message **at the beginning of the application process**. Crafting the message first forces your student to see his or her unique value the way an admissions board will.

You want your student's applications to evoke the same sense of unity and purpose. The next exercise will show you how...

Exercise: Making The Muv

(30 minutes)

Goal: To help your child shape the Message of Unique Value.

Instructions: Have fun with this! This is the culmination of a lot of hard work on both your parts.

1. Help your child to come up with:

- **intention:** the word, or words, that your child most wants to be defined by, such as *excellence*, *daring*, or *dedicated* (from the previous examples).
- **achievement:** three or four achievements that best reveal your child's driving purpose in life.
- **purpose:** how your child hopes to lead, serve, or create in the future.

2. Work together to brainstorm several drafts that combine your child's core **intention, achievement,** and **purpose**. Then support your child to compose the thematic Message of Unique Value (Muv).

13

REFINING THE BRAND:

admissions power

HERE'S THE SINGLE greatest insight that will empower your student's admissions chances.

Colleges are selfish.

It may not be flattering, but it's true. Beyond the manicured campuses and the hallowed traditions, you'll see that colleges are not so different from any other self-interested and profit-wary institution. Universities spend millions of dollars on boosting their reputations above the competition, either by seeking private endowments or public contracts.

Colleges also do a lot of work to hide their weaknesses, which are seldom evident on their websites. By filling these needs, students have a direct access to admissions.

admissions power: find the colleges' needs

Look at any university brochure and you'll see how image-conscious universities are. There's the information that a school consciously shares in the approved literature, and then there's the college as it really exists, warts and all.

With your student, you want to discover the places where prospective schools fall short of their ideal self-image. You can do this by finding out:

- Where the college prides itself.
- Ways the college has a less-than-positive reputation, often in issues like lack of representation of certain groups, lack of cohesion of the student body, and gaps in student satisfaction.
- Ways a college is consciously trying to grow or augment its reputation, such as building a new department or trying to enhance bona fides in a particular field of study.

Professional consultants can lend a practiced eye for ways that different colleges are trying to shore up weak spots, but you can also find these opportunity points from:

- College review sites
- Student interviews
- University websites
- College prospectus books

Exercise: Finding the Colleges' Needs

(1 hour x 3 nights)

Goal: To empower your child in the application process

Instructions:
For each of your child's top choice schools, find opportunity points and keep a roster using a format like the one below.

University Name: _____

Ways the school needs to improve its image: _____

admissions power: fill the college's needs

All colleges have shortcomings they want to fix and bona fides they want to improve upon. If your student can find and fill those needs with proven skills and experience, putting this fact front and center will increase chances of acceptance exponentially.

Diversity may be a weak spot, and if your student has shown leadership in organizing and bridging communities, that will raise him far above the competition. Other weak spots for universities often center on academic reputation, campus unity, and technological edge.

A prospective school might be seeking science students for its new chemistry wing or creative writers for the new film department. By doing a little research and finding out about that new chemistry wing or film department, students can double their chances of acceptance. They can prove their value at filling colleges' unmet needs through their essays, short answers, portfolios, and letters of reference.

Exercise: Filling the College's Needs

(30 minutes)

Goal: To match your child's unique value to college needs.

Instructions: Create and complete a table like the one below.

COLLEGE NAME	THE COLLEGE'S WEAK SPOTS	YOUR STRENGTHS / EXPERIENCES THAT FILL THE GAP

Think Like An Admissions Officer:
Final Committee

You breathe a deep sigh as you sit down to meet with your admission committee colleagues. You're finally nearing the finish line. Obviously, legacy kids will get admitted first, then the star athletes. The university knows where its bread is buttered after all, since legacies and athletes fill the vital needs of funding and publicity.

Who's next? Who has the best chance of admission? That's simple. As you glance around the table at yourself and the other admissions advisors, you're really the protectors of reputation. If a college is obsessed with anything, it's obsessed with reputation.

It's your job to find the students who will enrich your institution, students whose passions and talents can fill the campus's needs and make the university stronger in ways no other student can.

The students who can convey that exchange are the ones who get in.

- -

14

POWERING THE BRAND:

value exchange

IF YOUR STUDENT can convincingly fill a college's gaps, he or she *will be accepted*, with an increased chance for scholarship aid.

I see those acceptances happen every year. We get 96% of our clients into their first-choice school, and **Value Exchange** is how we do it. (In the students' section we use the acronym **Smuve**, or **S**trong **M**essage of **U**nique **V**alue **E**xchange, to add a touch of humor.)

Value Exchange sharpens the Brand tool, the Message of Unique Value, into a cohesive, ironclad statement for each particular school.

Think of it like this:

- Unique Value is a broad, branded statement of identity.
- Value Exchange fits the unique needs of each school.
- Unique Value makes your student a standout at any college.
- Value Exchange makes your student the perfect fit for each school.

We recommend that students include their respective theme of value in as many places as possible in their applications. Research shows that it takes at least four repetitions for a message to stick, so make sure your student hits the point of value exchange this many times, if not more.

By spotlighting value exchange on each application, students convince admissions officers of three critical factors:

- They are **highly committed** to their school.
- They are **prepared to thrive** on campus.
- They will strengthen their university *in ways no one else can.*

Here are two stories of students that did just that.

Julia from San Francisco, California

Unique Value: Bridge builder, talented scientist
College Need: More female representation in the sciences
Value Exchange: Representing women in science

Julia had many strengths as a student, including a talent for scientific study. During her sophomore year, she conducted an internship at a biomedical research institute, and entered an Intel Science competition. Among her other strengths were leadership, service as class president at her school, and tutoring fellow students in math and science.

When she began researching different universities, we found numerous gaps, especially ones involving women in the fields of science and math. Combining her passion for science and leadership, along with other skills made Julia a fantastic candidate for all of the schools she applied to.

Result: Admission to Whitman College, with a $60,000 scholarship.

Stephen from Los Angeles, California

Unique Value: Marketing genius, skilled organizer
College Need: Better diversity of LGBT students
Value Exchange: LGBT bridge-builder

Though we typically work with undergraduate admissions, Stephen contacted us trying to get into business school. As an undergrad, Stephen led organizations that unified LGBT communities on campus and raised awareness nationally for gay and lesbian struggles.

After college, he helped LGBT businesses improve their online presences through creative marketing strategies. Working with him, we explored different MBA programs and found that while most mentioned enhancing ethnic diversity, very few discussed LGBT diversity. Sensing a gap, Stephen utilized his marketing and bridge-building skills to make sure his application and essay echoed his theme of diversity.

Result: Full scholarships to the MBA programs at USC Marshall and University of Miami.

15

APPLYING THE BRAND:

strategic application

strategic application: the essays

Admissions officers want to know who students are, challenges they faced, and obstacles they overcame. The essay sections of applications give students that golden chance to express who they are in their own words, along with what they love and what they want out of life.

After grades and test scores, the essay decides the fate of your application more than anything else, so you want to make it count. The essay is what it all comes down to.

Great essays convey a student's fire for learning in living color, through vivid images and honest emotions that elucidate one's driving purpose in life and the message of unique value.

Generally, colleges give you two types of essays, a **main essay** and a **supplemental essay**. (Most private colleges and some public schools use the Common Application.)

1. **The Main Essay:**
   - gets sent to multiple schools.
   - expresses unique value and why your child is an excellent candidate for any college.
   - is built upon your child's Message of Unique Value (*Muv*)

2. **The Supplemental Essay:**
   - is unique to each school.
   - expresses the value exchange and why your student is a perfect match for a particular university.
   - is built around the Value Exchange (*Smuve*) Statement

For both essays, students want to avoid boasting, using gimmicks, adding "fluff," and claiming skills or ambitions they haven't developed. Admissions officers are trained to spot these tactics and to discard the applications that use them.

Colleges are searching for mature and developed candidates, so the winning path for both essays is for students to emphasize their unique value with a glimpse of who they are and why their presence matters. The applications will offer several prompts. If your student feels inspired by one of the given prompts, then go for it! However, if the given prompts feel stilted or boring, **don't force it.** Keep in mind two things:

- Essays make or break an application.
- Admissions officers rate the essays by your student's passion and excitement, not how well they answer the particular prompt.

When in doubt, we advise students to write about an experience that is most compelling or meaningful to them, and then find a way to tie the experience back to a prompt.

The essay is your student's chance to put their stamp on all of their hard work, sacrifice, and maturity. This is the time to savor the big achievements. Have fun with writing the essay and the essay will take care of itself.

Exercise: Essay Preparation

(1 hour)

Goal: To convey your child's fire to admissions officers

Instructions: For the **main essay**, which is sent to multiple universities, the main theme should be your child's Message of Unique Value (*the Muv Statement*).

For the **supplemental essay**, which is unique to each school, the main theme should be your child's Value Exchange with that particular school (*the Smuve Statement*).

---

strategic application: tailor each application

Colleges can tell when they're getting treated like a number and they don't appreciate it. Unfortunately, most students neglect to tailor their applications. They copy and paste the same information for every college, treating their first application as if it's their last.

We like to say that what's true for dating is true for admissions. If you want the colleges to like you, you have to make them feel special. Every school expects to be treated—and needs to be treated—like it's your child's first choice, and the way to do that is to **personalize**.

Personalizing means ordering responses for extracurriculars, honors, and awards in a way that highlights Value Exchange for each particular college.

Let's say a student wins five awards in high school:

- Varsity Football Team Manager
- Photography Portfolio Award, grand prize runner-up
- Perfect attendance record
- "Creative Rising Star" award from the local paper
- GPA ranked 4th in class

In random order, this list doesn't offer a clear thematic vision of who this student is. Ordering achievements in such a way is a waste of crucial space. But by approaching this list strategically, these same accomplishments can be arranged to create a compelling argument of value exchange.

Imagine this student is applying to a Division I school that is trying to improve its cultural reputation. This student could personalize a message of **artistic** value exchange by using the following order:

- Photography Award, grand prize runner-up
- "Creative Rising Star" award from the local paper
- GPA ranked 4th in class
- Perfect attendance record
- Varsity Football Team Manager

With this order, we see a creative young person who is both academically driven and able to relate to the wider community. Most importantly, we advise students to list their strongest accomplishments more than once and to keep them near the top regardless. Then they should list the experiences and achievements that best support the message of value exchange.

Exercise: Tailoring the Application

(1 hour)

Goal: To customize the applications to best fit each school

Instructions: Make sure your child knows to tailor applications.

strategic application: stay on message

In successful movies, every scene builds on the main overarching theme. The same is true with successful applications. Anything that clouds the story or muddles the message has to be taken out.

Unfortunately, many students pile on too much information, hoping that it will make them appear more accomplished. They do so much good work, but then at the last minute, flee from their message out of fear that it's not good enough. It's an understandable mistake, but a costly one.

Admissions boards get stacks and stacks of applications every day. They have too much to read already. By staying on message, your student will make sure that themes of uniqueness and value exchange shine through the entire application, so that admissions reps will surely take notice, no matter how worn out they may be.

The exercise that follows will help your student do just that.

Exercise: Stay on Message

(30 minutes)

Goal: To make sure that all information strengthens the Brand.

Instructions: Make sure your child knows to stay on message, using experiences which build a clear picture of unique value.

strategic application: explain low grades & scores

When students have academic weak spots, like low test scores or a GPA below 3.0, they need to:

1. Explain the factors that caused the low score
2. Show constructive efforts taken to improve their marks

Every application provides a section where students, if necessary, can state—in an honest and mature way—valid reasons why they performed below average.

You don't want to complain or blame others for low marks (especially a teacher), and you want to make sure any explanations given are valid:

Valid Explanations	Invalid Explanations
+ Learning disability	- Lousy teacher
+ Language barriers (for immigrants)	- Didn't like subject
+ Serious medical issues	- Light medical ailments
+ Socio-economic challenges	
+ Family challenges	

Students can freely admit that they weren't serious enough about academics or that they had a hard time with a subject. What's important is that students express a committed effort to improve by getting tutored, retaking a class, attending test-prep classes, or any other way they tried to correct low performance.

Colleges aren't looking for perfection. What they want to see is dedication and maturity and the will to address weaknesses and make improvements. It's okay if students don't have high marks across the board, long as they can show they did their best.

Exercise: Explain Low Grades and Scores

(1 hour)

Goal: To constructively address all low grades or test scores

Instructions: Make sure your child knows to explain any low grades or scores in a mature and thoughtful manner.

applying the brand: early application

Students apply early to let universities know that their school is at the top of their list. When students have their heart set on a particular school, we recommend applying early, especially if the school is selective or highly selective. Before applying, make sure you become familiar with the different methods of early application and how each one works.

1. **Early Decision**

   When you apply **early decision**, you make a morally binding agreement that if you get accepted, you'll go there and nowhere else. Students should only use **early decision** for their dream schools, because if they get in, they can't go anywhere else, even if they get accepted to a "better" option. The only valid excuses for getting out of the contract are financial in nature, such as if a student got accepted but didn't receive the financial aid she needed to attend.

   While it is *possible* to get out of the agreement—it isn't legally or financially binding—trying to void an early decision acceptance can be dicey.

2) **Early Decision *Two***

   Some private colleges offer a second round of early decision, for students who apply early decision but get turned down and then want to apply early to their second-favorite school.

3) Early Action

Many schools offer **early action.** Unlike early decision, early action isn't binding in any way.

4) Restricted Early Action

Like early action, **restricted early action** isn't binding, but the *restricted* part means that you agree not to apply early admission anywhere else. (Stanford and Harvard are two examples out of a handful of schools that use REA.)

Exercise: Early Application

(1 hour)

Goal: To decide if your child should apply early

Instructions: If your child has a dream school above all the rest, look into ways to apply early.

---

applying the brand: letters of recommendation

Most private colleges want two letters of recommendation. Public schools vary, from two recommendations to none at all. Letters of recommendation should be considered part of the whole application. Just like the essays, academic data, and short answers, effective letters need to highlight the application theme of **unique value** since references will send the same letter to each school.

Colleges that ask for two letters typically want one from a **humanities teacher** (English, history, the arts) and the other from a **math** or **science teacher.** When possible, we recommend this combination, but what's most important is that whoever gives the reference feels enthusiastic about your child's talents and abilities.

Students should approach prospective letter writers at least two months before applications are due. Three months is even better. Students should approach references and cordially ask if they're willing to write an **enthusiastic letter of recommendation.** If a reference hesitates in the slightest or seems at all unwilling, **find someone else to write the letter.**

Next, students should provide each reference with a **Reference Helper Sheet,** which outlines the student's theme of unique value and lists the important achievements that highlight that theme. **Teachers appreciate this direction**, as it gives them a structure around which to frame their letter.

Once the applications are sent, students will want to call or email the admissions offices to make sure that letters of recommendation and other application materials have all been received. Finally, once the letters have been sent, make sure to thank references for their time with a nice note or small gift.

Exercise: Letters of Recommendation

(1 hour)

Goal: To make sure your child receives strong letters of recommendation.

Instructions: Be sure your child finds letter writers who are enthusiastic, and supply them with your child's unique value statement and a supporting list of experiences and accomplishments. This will ensure that the letters serve to highlight the themes of unique value.

BRAND U

The Brand for Parents In a Nutshell

- Create a **master list** of all your child's experiences and achievements since 9th grade.

- Craft a *Muv Statement*, the brand that conveys your child's fire of vision and purpose.

- Empower your child's position in the application process by finding the needs of each particular school.

- Explore the ways your child has the skills and experience to fill needs of prospective schools. **Value exchange** can more than double your child's chances of admission.

- The *Smuve Statement* details why your child is a perfect fit for each particular school, by molding your student's unique value into a proposition of value that resonates with each college's specific need.

- Write **essays** from the most inspiring prompts. **Main essays** go to each university and convey unique value, while **supplemental essays** are tailored for each school and convey value exchange.

- **Personalize** extracurriculars, honors, achievements, and short answers to each particular school to convey value exchange.

- **Stay on message** by making sure every element in the application serves to spotlight unique value and value exchange.

- If interested in **early application**, know the options and deadlines.

- Approach letter writers **two months** before application deadlines, and make sure they're *enthusiastic.*

CASE STUDY: JULIA

I THOUGHT IT would be helpful for you to see the positioning process in action, so I'm sharing the story of a real client so that you can judge for yourself.

Julia became a College Match client as a junior at an inner-city high school. Born in Mexico, Julia was raised in a single-parent household with four siblings, and aspired to be the first person in her family to attend college.

During our initial consultation, College Match observed much academic and social strength in Julia's credentials, including a 3.9 GPA. Julia was a well-organized student who was socially and politically active at her school, and she had thought about running for class office. On the other side, we saw that Julia faced challenges in her standardized testing, with her PSAT score at 950.

Part I: Catching the Sparks

At College Match, our first obligation is to gain a deep and thorough understanding of our client's needs, hopes, and desires for life. We conduct a series of interviews with students and their parents to get a sense of who a student is and what they want out of life. We pose questions like:

- *If you only had one goal in life, what would you like to accomplish?*
- *What specific steps will help you achieve this goal?*

- *What are the top six values and principles that drive your decisions in life?*
- *How would you like people in the future to perceive you: academically? socially? professionally?*

In Julia's case, her goals in life include "to help my fellow Latinos" and "become a respected leader" or "a professional in my community."

Part II: Building Fire

By the time we met Julia, she had already begun building a strong record of value. During her sophomore year, she had coached junior varsity volleyball, and had worked the summer before junior year assisting in the creation of a pre-teen volunteering program called Helping Hands through her Lutheran Church (for which the church awarded her the volunteer of the year award).

Academically, she had registered for the academic enhancement organization, Upward Bound, where she won the Gregor Mendel Award for meticulous scholarship in genetics. She also worked as an administrative intern for Seattle Biomedical Research Institute.

Step 1: Building on Julia's Leadership Value

Real world experience: College Match recommended that Julia support her scientific interests and abilities by conducting scientific research in the real world. We helped identify an internship at the Biomedical Institute and pointed her toward conducting her own research experiments in biotech. College Match also discussed the possibility of entering, for example, the Intel Science competition. Follow-up included researching local science and biotechnology organizations with high school research programs, including a university cancer research center. We also looked for summer camps in science and engineering at Ivy-level schools that supported Julia's interest in science and technology.

Student Leadership: We encouraged Julia to run for class president her senior year. Though she was initially uncertain of her capacity to get elected, once she put herself into the contest, her passion for leadership took over and she was successfully voted into office.

Celebrating Uniqueness: As a first-generation Mexican American, Julia had experienced challenges overcoming her lack of fluency in English. College Match reviewed her life visions to help fellow Latinos, become a respected leader, and a professional in her community. We advised Julia to look into tutoring her fellow students in ESL, whereby she could provide a service, build personal value, and spend several hours each week brushing up on her own writing and editing skills.

Additionally, we encouraged her to find other ways of celebrating her identity. Julia did this by teaching Latin dance classes at her church. Lastly, her family had faced challenges financially. Again, Julia used this adversity to prove her resilience and leadership value, helping to run a local chapter of a nonprofit that provided low-income students with formal wear for weddings, proms, graduations, and other major events.

Summer bridge programs: Another recommendation we gave to Julia was to prove that she could succeed away from home in a university setting. Schools are often concerned that students who have little experience away from home might fall apart when they arrive at college. Therefore, College Match identified and helped Julia apply to a number of summer bridge programs, including programs at Carleton College, Carnegie Mellon University, Brown, Stanford, and other summer enrichment programs, such as marine science at UC Santa Barbara. One criteria for reviewing these programs included looking for places offering environmental science courses.

Step 2: Balancing Out Weak Spots
a) Writing Skills
Julia's writing was not as strong as it needed to be for a top-tier liberal arts college or university. This factor was largely due to the fact that her first language was Spanish. While her writing in English was adequate for high school, College Match believed that Julia needed to improve reading and writing to catch the attention of some writing-oriented competitive colleges. College Match contacted several summer writing programs and managed to obtain a writing tutor (an English professor) from University of Washington to assist Julia with her summer writing study including composition and grammar. We also recommended a summer reading list complete with SAT "vocabulary novels" offering advanced vocabulary including, 200 or so likely-to occur words on the SAT.

b) Low SAT and ACT Scores
Our initial consultation with Julia uncovered a major weakness in the area of standardized testing: her PSAT score was just below 1000 and her ACT score was 21 composite. Upward Bound scheduled her to take the SAT in June. Instead, College Match recommended that Julia take a practice SAT to generate a baseline score. If the score wasn't above 1200, College Match advised her to wait and enroll in a SAT prep course.

Part III: Choosing the U

Step 3: Choosing the Optimal Undergraduate Experience
Working with College Match, Julia decided that she wanted a close-knit campus offering the type of hands-on, personal instruction that a smaller liberal arts college would afford her. She had seen older friends win scholarships to large research universities, only to get lost in the crowd and drop out.

Already facing the challenge of living away from home for the first time, she wanted to be at a college where she'd be more than a number. Moreover, one of her life visions was to return home to be a leader and defender of her community, something she could accomplish by getting a medical degree. Combining all of these reasons, along with communicating effectively and a proven track record of helping other students take leadership roles, a small liberal arts college stood out as Julia's optimal undergraduate experience.

Step 4: Making the Informed Choice
Working with College Match, Julia explored different liberal arts colleges to find the right fit, ranking her favorites by quality of education, student care, campus culture, real-world preparation. She researched metrics such as class size, percentage of freshman students retained, campus diversity, and medical school placement. Financial aid was also a big consideration, so she rated different schools by the types of merit-based aid each provided.

Step 5: College Visits
College Match scheduled college visits for Julia that were designed to help her get the "feel" for college life. College Match contacted admission offices of colleges to organize overnight stays and classroom visits at Reed, Claremont McKenna, Occidental, and Whitman.

Step 6: Creating the "I" List
For each college she was applying to, Julia wrote out an "I" list, answering the question "Why I want to attend college X." Then, for each college, College Match helped Julia develop an argument based on her strengths that she would bring to the colleges, as well as her needs.

Part IV: Applying the Brand

Step 7: Creating Julia's Message of Unique Value (Muv Statement)
Working with our clients, the first step of the application process is to develop a central theme that will clearly convey a student's unique value to admissions officers. Julia's central theme was "leadership." She would be the first in her family to attend a four-year college. She had created a pre-teen volunteer outreach program at her church, and she had led at her school as class president. Her numerous extracurriculars supported her passion for leadership, from helping to create community at her school as senior class president to tutoring other students in math and science, from teaching Brazilian dance classes to running a local nonprofit that provides prom dress rentals for low-income students.

Taking the central theme one step further, we created this Muv Statement: "In every facet of her life, Julia evokes leadership to raise the quality of her surroundings, from student leadership and dedication to academics, and a proven commitment to supporting her family and community."

Step 8: Pinpointing College Needs
a) Finding the colleges' needs
During each college visit, College Match asked Julia to speak with at least 10 students, asking each of them about what they liked and disliked most about their college. We also had her research a recent college prospectus to see where statistical data had fluctuated. Students' dislikes helped to define each college's weak points.

b) Filling the colleges' needs
Julia discovered that several of the colleges on her list hoped to increase ethnic diversity but at the same time worried about interaction among students of differing ethnic, social, and economic backgrounds. College Match coached Julia to address this need by showcasing her leadership

as class president and her unique value as a community and cultural leader. Moreover, she shared examples of "community building" and personal pride in her leadership organizing the Formal Wear Exchange for low-income students. All of these roles required her to bring together students from differing circumstances to achieve goals.

Julia also found that a few of the schools felt that women were underrepresented in their science departments, and thus were making a major effort to increase the number of women in their science majors.

Step 9: Expressing Julia's Key Value Exchange
a) Personalizing each application
College Match helped Julia organize each college application by theme, emphasizing Julia's key value exchange for each particular school. Several schools had issues surrounding diversity of the student body, so Julia crafted a message of unique value exchange to show her "leadership as a community builder and cultural bridge," and used her experiences of student leadership, volunteer coordination, and activities celebrating her cultural heritage to highlight this point.

Other schools were trying to improve representation of women in the sciences, so Julia tailored a Strong Message of Unique Value Exchange, or *Smuve*, to highlight her "leadership in scientific achievement and community outreach." As evidence, she provided her winning the Trailblazer Award in science, her experiences tutoring other students in math and science, her leadership in student government, and other experiences as a leader for her community.

b) Interview prep
College Match conducted mock interviews to prepare Julia for meeting with admissions representatives. Part of the mock interview included determining her best argument for admission and her key value exchange as a first-generation Mexican-American with leadership

qualifications, academic interests (sciences and sociology), her research in biotechnology, and community building by bringing different groups together.

b) Essay development

College Match counseled Julia to write about a pivotal moment. She chose a very personal moment involving considerable personal and emotional trauma. Normally, an essay would focus on the positive aspects of a client's life. In this case, however, a moment of great personal anguish provided a clearer picture of Julia's emotional strength and resolve. Through her perseverance, the reader could draw a very clear picture of this student's character and leadership abilities.

c) Contacting Letter Writers

With our guidance, Julia chose letter writers who could give high enthusiasm and special insight into Julia's high school career. Using our format, Julia contacted her letter writers and provided them with an outline containing her Muv Statement and the value highlighting her academic strength, scientific achievement, school leadership, and community outreach.

The Result:

The Brand U strategy proved to be a rousing success for Julia.

Whitman College, Mt. Holyoke, Evergreen, University of Puget Sound, *and* University of Washington all accepted Julia. At the time of her acceptances, she also won an undergraduate science achievement award and a $3000 Boeing and MESA scholarship for women going into science and engineering.

The principal of her high school awarded her a scholarship for $2,000, and another community member donated a new laptop computer. Ultimately, Julie chose her first choice, Whitman College, where she was awarded a merit scholarship of $15,000 each year.

STUDENTS

SECTION

PART V

SPARKS
Fire
Vision
Brand

Who are you?

What do you love?

What do you want out of life?

WELCOME TO THE College Selection and Admissions Process.

Do the words *research, achievement tests, prep classes,* and *applications:*

  a) Turn your stomach
  b) Bore you to tears
  c) Sound like zero fun
  d) All of the above

Have faith. We're here to help. All we need is one hour of your time a week. You don't even have to do this every week, just two weekends a month. In return, you'll find a great college that will prepare you for a life you'll love.

This book has one goal: to make sure that when you finish college in a few years, you'll look back and feel gratitude and fulfillment about your college experience.

Your words become your actions,

Your actions become your values,

Your values become your destiny.

Gandhi

16

ORIGINAL SPARKS:

the story of your life

WHEN STUDENTS APPLY to college, the admissions officers see test scores and read the essays and short answers. Together, it plays out in their minds like a movie. Colleges get thousands of applications each year, and they decide whose movie is most compelling and most deserving of acceptance.

The admissions reader's perspective is important. But there's a critic that's far more important than any college: you. After all, you'll be the one watching the movie of your life for decades to come.

We're talking about memories. Whether we like them or not, they play out day after day, all through our lives. Memories can tell us that we're capable of doing great things with our lives, or they can do the opposite. They can make us feel proud and grateful to be who we are, or they can leave us regretful and defeated.

That's why right now is so important. Today might seem like just another day in the life, but today's actions become tomorrow's memories.

We want you to love the movie of your life. Colleges want to love your movie too. They aren't looking for perfection—far from it. What captures their imagination are young people who have faced their fears and triumphed over their limitations, students who have defined what they love and pursued it with passion, maturing through challenges in the heroic transformation of adolescence to adulthood. Heroes aren't perfect, but they succeed in the most important way: by discovering their uniqueness and becoming themselves.

This book makes one request: that you give yourself the small investment of time that the Brand U method asks of you. You'll still have plenty of time for friends, fun, and all the things you love to do, but give these memories that you'll create your time as well. After all, you'll be living with them for months, years, and decades to come.

So be a friend to your future self. Only one person is unique enough to get you admitted into the life you dream of having, and that's you.

Exercise: Finding the Sparks

(30 minutes)

Goal: To pinpoint your unique talents and interests

Instructions: List all of the experiences, teams, clubs, hobbies, and more that you've gotten the greatest sense of satisfaction from. For each experience, explore what you liked best and what talents you enjoyed developing.

17

CREATING SPARKS:

starting the journey

WHETHER YOU KNOW it or not, you're at the beginning of a great journey. The good news is that you're in control. The voyage is yours to take.

You have many challenges before you. High school is a battery of facing obstacles, passing tests, making friends, finding love, pleasing your parents, graduating...and way down the line, towering like a mountain in the distance, lies the final hurdle of getting into college.

Right now, you've got a heap of other things to worry about, not the least of which is a midterm or an SAT or a job or research paper, or the fact that your friends, coaches, teachers, and parents all have expectations of you to be a certain person, which may or may not be who you really are.

Who exactly are you?

As a high school student, you have to contend with the conflicting expectations of parents, teachers, and peers, and perhaps even coaches, religious leaders, and bosses. Then there are the expectations we get from movies, television, and the Internet. With so many people telling us who to be, how in the world are we supposed to figure it out for ourselves?

It's understandable that so many students take the pre-drawn paths. At every high school across the country, students assume the labels given to them by their teachers and peers—jock, computer geek, math whiz, etc. There's nothing bad about adopting the mold as a way to survive.

The problem is that a mold becomes very confining. Do you want to live the rest of your life confined to a type, or would you like to thrive as a uniquely self-defined individual?

That's what this journey is about. It's a journey that only you can take. Nothing could be more difficult. It takes courage. It takes a hero.

That's you.

You bring an exclusive combination of talents and interests that you—and only you—possess. In these sparks lie your potential, the promise of finding your dream college and the life you can create from there.

Getting into college is challenging, but it doesn't have to be stressful.

If you find out who you are, what you love, and pursue it with a passion, then regardless of what happens, you'll gain admission into the life you want to live.

Exercise: Seeking Guidance

(30 minutes)

Goal: To get advice from a mentor

Instructions: Interview your three favorite mentors (teachers, coaches, instructors, employers, etc.) and tell them you're planning the future. Trust us, they'll be happy to help.

Tell them your hopes for the future, and ask them how they think you can reach those aspirations. Ask them what they see as your talents, ways you can grow, and what specific steps you can begin taking to achieve your hopes and goals.

PART VI

Sparks
FIRE
Vision
Brand

IN THE SPARKS section, we began exploring your unique talents and interests. We dive into those pursuits to build a fire of vision and purpose that will prepare you for the coming challenges of selecting and getting into college.

You'll be tested many times on your journey ahead, but that's okay. Every good adventure has to have some obstacles, and if you can capture and build upon the spark of your uniqueness, everything will fall into place. You'll find yourself with a vision of the future and the college you want to go to.

Mistakes and failures are inevitable. They're our best teachers along the way. In fact, the stories that win colleges over are found in how you overcome the limitations and setbacks you face. This is your opportunity to take control of our own identity and determine who you are and who you'll become.

So, let's get this fire started.

18

IGNITING FIRE:

discovering intentions

TO MAXIMIZE YOUR opportunities moving forward, we'll locate your hopes and dreams and dig down to find the wellspring of your deepest intentions in life. This is the fuel that will light the fire and propel you forward in life.

In the table below, there's a list of example hopes and dreams at the top, and below each one, the surface ambitions versus the deeper ambitions.

Table 4.1—Example Life Goals of Students

	Famous celebrity	*Famous Software Developer*	*Nobel Prize Winner—Science*
Expressed Ambition	To be famous	To be rich and powerful	To be remembered and celebrated
Underlying Social Ambition	To make people happy	To make people's lives easier	To help the world in some major way
Underlying Personal Ambition	To perform	To invent, make dreams a reality	To be a leader in scientific discovery

These are natural ambitions students often have, and it's helpful to probe the underlying intentions:

Being a **professional singer** is appealing in many ways, for the pleasure of being sought after and famous, just to name two reasons. However, the desire for fame is hardly a good motivator (or nearly everyone would be famous). Looking more closely, we find that beneath fame, there are heartfelt desires: to make people happy and to express creativity through performance. These intentions can be lived out in many positive ways and can bring great satisfaction, whether on the stage or off.

Being a **successful software developer** would allow one to be rich and powerful. However, that desire hardly achieves anything, or else we'd all be billionaires. On the other hand, the ambition to improve people's lives and to pursue invention can spark a journey to success that can take many different forms and drive unique growth opportunities.

Being a **Nobel Prize winner in science** sounds appealing, for the honor of being remembered and celebrated. But on a deeper and more meaningful level, this desire is rooted in the twin ambitions of helping the world in some major way and pursuing scientific discovery, both of which can be developed in many different ways.

The exercise below will help you dig beneath the surface of your hopes and dreams, to locate the core values and ambitions that make you who you are and hold the promise of the life you can create.

Exercise: Fueling the Sparks

(30 minutes)

Goal: To find the deep ambitions that will drive growth

Instructions: Fill in the table below based on your best answers.

	Life Hope #1 ____	Life Hope #2 ____	Life Hope #3 ____
Surface Ambition			
Deep Service Ambition			
Deep Personal Ambition			

19

CATCHING FIRE:

transformative paths

THE WORLD OFTEN tries to put us in categories whether we like it or not: jock, brain, band nerd, geek, and so on. But by building a fire inside, you determine who you are and what you want out of life.

This is an internal fire, fueled by the sparks of your talents and interest, and it provides the vision and purpose that will propel you to the life you dream of having. For nearly two decades, I've helped hundreds of young people turn their unique sparks of talent and interest into fire through four specific paths:

- Leadership
- Entrepreneurship
- Service
- Creativity

What follows are stories of young people who did just that, young people who took the sparks of their unique talents and interests and built a fire of inspiration.

They were ordinary kids at their high schools, labeled as jocks, artists, tech geeks, and science nerds. But these kids refused to be typecast. Instead, they created a unique identity by defining what they loved and who they wanted to become.

As you read about them, find inspiration in imagining what you could achieve if you let your talents and passions run wild. Imagine if, like them, you created your own identity and claimed it as your own.

Joseph from Phoenix, Arizona

High School Label: "Tennis Jock"
Sparks: Love of tennis, gregarious, friendly
Catching Fire: Leadership

Joseph came to us as a sophomore in high school, a good student and competitive tennis player in Phoenix, Arizona, but with little development of other skills. Together, we sought ways that he could use his passion for tennis to develop skills of leadership and encouraged him to look for ways he could serve the needs of his community.

In the spring of 10th grade, Joseph contacted his local Boys and Girls Club and learned that Phoenix had few summer programs to help inner city youth stay out of trouble, so Joseph created a plan for a tennis clinic for low-income children in the area. Working with his parents, he visited local pro shops, got sponsors for his clinic, and acquired used racquets and balls for the kids. Next, he worked with the local Boys and Girls club to secure tennis courts. That summer, Joseph's camp grew in popularity, increasing from just eight kids the first week to fifty by the end of the summer. We urged Joseph to take his success and scale it upwards, and during his junior year, Joseph wrote a handbook on how to start tennis clinics in other areas. The following summer, Joseph expanded his inner city tennis program to two other cities.

Discovered Brand: Community leader, civic entrepreneur

Ali from Santa Clara, California

High School Label: Teacher's Pet
Sparks: Compassion, love of people
Catching Fire: Entrepreneurship

We began working with Ali as a ninth grader. She was unsure of her talents, but she had a great interest in her family origins in Bucharest, Romania. It occurred to us that she had the gift of compassion and a love of her people. The following summer, she volunteered at an orphanage for Romanian children, and became so taken with the children's needs that when she began high school in Silicon Valley, she organized a club to raise awareness. In the following two years, she put on fundraisers to illustrate how financial support could have a meaningful, long-lasting impact on these children in need.

With each year, she gained confidence in her role, bringing awareness to her community and raising over $20,000 to improve living conditions for the Romanian children in need.

Discovered Brand: Nonprofit entrepreneur

Peter from Berkeley, California

High School Label: "Art Geek"
Sparks: Love of art, Creative, Inspired
Catching Fire: Service

When we started working with Peter, he expressed few interests except for drawing and designing models in his back yard. Given his interests and talents, we suggested that he explore ways to use his sparks for the good of others. By chance, Peter's father had contacts with a charitable NGO that built homes in Guatemala.

In 10th grade, Peter applied for a work visa and spent the next summer learning how the homes were designed and built. When he returned home, he spent his junior year applying his passion to drafting blueprints. The following summer, he implemented the plans that he had formulated and gained incredible confidence and satisfaction in watching his designs become homes for needy Guatemalans.

Discovered Brand: Architect

George from Sacramento, California

High School Label: "Class Clown"
Sparks: Lyrical talent, love of music
Catching Fire: Creativity

As a junior, George came to us with a great deal of uncertainty over what he could offer. He wasn't interested in extracurriculars, and had few interests beyond hip hop music. Instead of forcing him into fields he wasn't interested in, we encouraged him to see if he could use his musical skills to fill any needs in his school and community.

George noted that many of his fellow students were struggling in pre-calculus, so the following summer, he harnessed his creative talents, wrote, and used his home equipment to produce hip hop songs that taught fundamentals of calculus in a way that young students could relate to and understand. His efforts won recognition at his school and his work became an online sensation that schools across the country used.

Discovered Brand: Music Producer

- -

Exercise: Building Fire

(30 minutes)

Goal: To choose a transformative path for self-discovery

Instructions: Make a sheet with three columns, with one listing your sparks and another listing your deep ambitions.

Think about the needs of your school and community, and working with your parents and other mentors, list ways to apply your sparks through leadership, entrepreneurship, service, and creativity, and put them in the third column. **Pick your favorite two options**, and get help from parents and teachers to make and execute a plan.

20

BUILDING FIRE:

transformative experience

IN CHAPTER 3, we explored ways to set your sparks afire through unique paths of transformation. Here, we move forward to explore more ways to help you develop qualities of leadership, service, entrepreneurship, and creativity.

While working with students, we've found that the following are excellent ways to further define your passions and skills:

- University programs
- Personalized employment
- Competitions and scholarships
- Research
- International experience
- Publishing and performance

transformative experience: university programs

Getting collegiate-level instruction while in high school is a great way to build on your strongest talents and interests. Most major universities offer study programs to high school students in various fields of interest.

University programs offer you a collegiate atmosphere and the experience of learning away from parents and home. Additionally, you can study under highly-trained professors who can help you accelerate your development in your favorite fields through research and publishing.

Jenny from Manhattan, New York

High School Label: "Emo Bohemian"
Sparks: Passion for writing, persistence
Building Fire: University program

When we met Jenny, she was a sophomore and an aspiring poet. With this in mind, we urged her to submit her work to various summer programs, and she won entrance into the prestigious University of Iowa's Young Writer's Workshop, where she spent the summer developing her work under published authors.

With their guidance, she returned home with a polished portfolio, which she submitted to multiple competitions. The following school year, she continued her development as a writer, traveling cross-country to deliver poetry readings in Ithaca, NY and at Hugo House in Seattle. That spring, she was awarded a national Scholastic Award for creative writing. The following year, with these credits, she gained admission to the highly-regarded English programs at Cornell and Sarah Lawrence.

Brand: Published Author

transformative experience: personalized employment

Jobs are a great way to develop confidence and maturity while building your talents in your field of interest. But don't settle for a random job because it's easy or with your friends. If you have a passion for a certain area, find work that focuses on that passion, gives you a sense of purpose, and expands your horizons.

Bill from Honolulu, Hawaii

High School Label: "Dumb Jock"
Sparks: Positivity, leadership
Building Fire: Personalized employment

Bill began volunteering at a local YMCA in 9th grade and by his junior year, had become a student athletic director, organizing leagues and teaching basketball and indoor soccer to kids in after-school programs. During this time, one of the kids named Jack caught his attention, because he had a hard time following directions. After contacting Jack's family, Bill learned that the boy suffered from an acute case of autism.

While working with Bill on his college development, we advised him to research autism, and Bill got in touch with learning disability experts to find out ways to help Jack. Over time, he became a coach and mentor to Jack and other children who had learning challenges. The result was that his college essays revealed a high degree of maturity and compassion, and won him admission and merit award offers at Haverford, Whitman, and Lewis and Clark.

Brand: Community Leader, Mentor

transformative experience: competitions & scholarships

Every year, literally thousands of medals and scholarships are awarded to students in every field of learning. Even just taking part gives constructive validation that you're willing to aspire to a high level of achievement. The following stories illustrate how participating in competitions and winning scholarships can provide exactly the type of third-party validation that colleges look for.

Paula from Florence, Italy

High School Label: "Science Nerd"
Sparks: Love of science, courage
Building Fire: Unique competition

When we met Paula, we asked her which adults she admired, and she described her grandfather, a doctor. From a young age, he'd captivated her imagination with his descriptions of surgery and healing the sick. As she entered high school, Paula discovered a passion for science, and physiology in particular, and so we encouraged her to pursue ways to explore these areas outside of school.

The summer after 10th grade, she worked at a local blood bank, which led to her applying and getting accepted to Oxford University hospital as an intern her junior year. While there, she worked directly under doctors studying links between cancer and red meat consumption.

When she came home, she submitted a paper on her experiences, which won a state science fair competition, an achievement that testified to her passion for medical research and her vision to become a doctor. Because of this, she gained entrance into an elite premedical program at Tufts University in Boston.

Brand: Healer

----

transformative experience: research

Research is an excellent way to fuel passion and talent. It presents opportunities to work closely with a professional mentor in a variety of fields, from science to history, and math to journalism, just to name a few.

Conducting research teaches technical skills and discipline that push your talents to a higher level, creates legitimacy, and helps you focus in on the specific life goals you want to pursue.

Tariq from Los Angeles, California

High School Label: "Foreign Kid"
Sparks: Passion for politics and human rights, strong reading skills
Building Fire: Unique research

Tariq was a sophomore in high school when we began working with him. Because of his core interests and talents, we urged him to study political science through a university program. He was accepted to Harvard's summer program, and chose to study the complex political situation in Pakistan. At Harvard, he began to amass research under a doctorate-level professor, who guided him towards writing a policy piece on the Barelvi movement in Pakistan.

With the help of our in-house writing advisor, Tariq developed his work, which won attention from the department chair of Harvard's Islamic Studies program, a noteworthy accomplishment which solidified his confidence and earned him acceptance at Columbia and the University of Chicago.

Brand: Political Scholar

transformative experience: unique international work/study

International work and study are fantastic routes for personal growth. You can literally expand your horizons through immersion into new and unfamiliar realities as you experience different cultures, learn new languages, and discover that the world is wilder than you imagined.

However, international experience has to be unique. Every year, thousands of well-meaning students venture abroad on volunteer programs, tutoring in orphanages, and cleaning up after floods. There's nothing wrong with that at all.

The only problem can be that the experiences are all pre-planned and very self-contained. Students in such programs seldom branch out beyond groups very similar to themselves, and rather than developing their unique talents, they end up playing a type much like the one they have back home. They go far away, only to come back home pretty much the same as when they had left.

We recommend students tailor their study and work abroad to their specific passions and interests. Before you go, set up a plan for the skills and experience you hope to gain and how you hope to do so. While abroad, be sure to journal or blog about the experience so you can bring your transformation back home. Document it online, using Google Docs, Flickr, YouTube, or whatever venue makes sense for how you want to express and share your journey.

Malika from Portland, Oregon

High School Label: "Tough Girl"
Sparks: A passion for social sciences and international affairs
Building Fire: Unique international work

We met Malika as a sophomore. Her parents were doctors and she had extended relatives living in Africa. During trips abroad, she experienced first-hand the HIV epidemic in Uganda, and came back determined to help. With our encouragement, she took courses at a local college and received guidance to begin a study on methods that could decrease infection rates, which gained recognition from a national online journal and attention from a Pan-African conference.

Her work helped solidify her passion and authenticity as an agent of change and service, and earned her admission and a merit-based scholarship to Occidental College. There, she majors in Diplomacy and World Affairs and is interning at the UN in New York.

Brand: International Aid Worker

----

transformative experience: publishing & performance
In a highly-competitive world, students who can voice their passion and publish or perform their talents stand out in maturity and power. It takes dedication to build your skills to a level of recognition, and it demands courage and poise to place your talents before the judgment of an audience.

If your path is writing, see if you can profile your experiences through a state, local, or even national publication, like a newspaper, magazine, or an online journal. If you're an actor, musician, or performer, try to create a show of your own, or join together with other performers. If you can't find a venue, create your own. Hold talent nights that create a sense of community and help others like you share their voice. Your mentors and teachers will be glad to assist.

If you're an artist, compile a portfolio and draft an artist's statement. Join with fellow artists and set up an exhibition in your hometown, featuring a series of a dozen or more of your best works. The experience of "professionalizing" your art before a live audience will take your passion to a higher level.

As with other experiences, it's fine if you perform through a school program, but you will grow exponentially by stepping out on your own and creating your own plan and performance vision.

Erika from Brooklyn, New York

High School Label: "Drama Geek"
Sparks: Creative passion, imagination, and dedication
Building Fire: Unique performance

When we interviewed Erika, we uncovered that her greatest ambition in life was "to express her creativity through the arts." Her interests revolved around writing and theater, so we encouraged her to try writing a play. With guidance from her English teacher and writing coaches, she wrote out a script based on her life in New York City.

After writing several drafts, her play was performed at her high school, and to her surprise, the play was widely accepted in her community as a great work. With this boost of confidence, she decided to take her story to a larger audience. Enlisting the support of her parents, friends, and fellow drama classmates, she held a fundraiser to get her classmates and herself to Scotland the following year. After a year of organizing, they performed their piece and won recognition at the Edinburgh Fringe Festival.

Discovered Brand: Playwright and Theatrical Producer

Tips for
Building Fire

- If interested in the health field, think about internships in hospitals, find health needs in the community and see if there are organizations that bring awareness, outreach, and support. Start there, and take it even further with research opportunities, or creating your own outreach group in your school or community.
- If interested in science, look for research opportunities via projects and for competitions and scholarships in math, engineering, and technology. Bridge and university programs can often be a great place to find mentoring and research opportunities. Another outlet is finding ways to apply special skills in math, finance, computer science, or engineering to social needs.
- If interested in finance or business, think about opportunities for entrepreneurship, and seek guidance from mentors. Look for opportunities to create a business or philanthropy, draft a proposal, and seek funding.
- If interested in sports, find ways to use your passion for athletics to help the underserved in your community, through youth programs, coaching, and leadership.
- If interested in the arts, explore ways to build a portfolio of your work through film, writing, and performance. Team up with others to create supportive environments, performance nights, gallery showings, and offer creative services to help others in unique ways.
- If interested in international relations and foreign cultures, explore *unique* work and study opportunities abroad. Before you go, be sure to create a plan, and afterwards, a statement, research paper, or article detailing what you learned, to be submitted for publication.

Exercise: Building Fire

(30 minutes)

Goal: To create the right transformative experiences for you

Instructions: Which experiences would you like to fuel your passion and talents? (Choose your **two favorite options**.)

- Summer university bridge programs
- Unique employment
- Academic competitions and scholarships
- Research projects
- International experience
- Publishing
- Portfolio development

Once you've chosen your favorites from above, work with your parents and teachers to match your sparks and ambitions to create paths of leadership, service, creativity, and entrepreneurship.

What specific steps will help you achieve your deep ambitions?

21

INSPIRING FIRE:

personal triumphs

LIFE IN HIGH school can be *very* difficult if you're "different." Yet, if you look past high school, the people who lead great lives in college and beyond are the ones who learned to celebrate their uniqueness early on.

We won't lie. It takes courage. Being different can get you mocked, teased, or worse. But remember, everyone has experienced the pain of adversity, if not first-hand then through a friend, classmate, or family member. Every day, people young and old struggle with adversity related to things like health issues, discrimination, poverty, and lack of social acceptance.

By facing adversity head-on and with courage, we can change ourselves and the world around us. Dig deep and be brave. Recognize the power of your uniqueness to change the world. Don't be afraid of the greatest gift you have.

The challenges we face make us who we are, and by facing and overcoming these challenges, we find our purpose in life and inspire those around us: our parents, our friends, our teachers, and yes, colleges as well.

Kara from San Diego, California

High School Label: "Lab Geek"
Sparks: Passion for science, sensitivity, generosity
Inspiring Fire: Health

While we didn't work with Kara as a client, her story was too inspiring to pass up. Growing up, Kara had watched her father and brother both suffer from diabetes. Having seen the ravages of the illness on her loved ones, she decided to dedicate herself to helping those with the disease. She excelled in biology classes, and received guidance to enroll in summer programs at a local university.

There, she worked in both the research lab and hospital, where she visited with diabetes patients. When she returned to school, she organized a diabetes awareness group at school, which then organized a week-long, school-wide forum to educate her peers on healthy eating habits and making healthy life choices. Her work garnered her recognition and entry into UC Berkeley, with a full scholarship.

Brand: Student Leader, Public Health Activist

Bryce from Olympia, Washington

High School Label: "Tribal Kid"
Sparks: Language talents, good with computers
Inspiring Fire: Cultural Heritage

When we began working with Bryce, he told us his vision was to become a software engineer. Bryce's father was a member of the

Cowlitz Tribe's General Counsel, but up to then, Bryce had only moderate involvement in tribal affairs. One of the challenges we found was that the tribe's numbers were in decline and that its language was in danger of extinction, in part because the language was kept in a book that few people had access to.

Bryce brainstormed ways he could help, and created a plan to digitize the language and storing it online so that the Tribe's members and linguists could have ready access for teaching. Bryce's language digitization project was born, combining his personal talent with cultural pride. By his senior year, a number of prestigious schools had already shown interest in having Bryce on their campus.

Brand: Linguist, Computer programmer

Wade from Kansas City, Missouri

High School Label: "Tech Dork"
Sparks: Love of computers, ingenuity and discipline
Inspiring Fire: Unique Interests

Wade, 16, claimed to have no extracurricular activities. Looking at where he spent his time out of class, we found no organized activities, sports, or clubs. On the other hand, he spent considerable time working on his computer, fixing things and even going so far as to build a computer from scraps like the motherboard that he recycled from discarded computers. He also painted model figures of warriors he'd dreamed up by himself.

His ability to build computers and work diligently to create an elaborate fantasy world were impressive to us, but Wade had always thought his talents meaningless since he got teased for them at school. With our encouragement, he began listing his products online for sale, and by junior year had started a business that was so profitable, he hired several employees by the following summer. His "unpopular" interests became the basis for social acceptance into a community which prized his talents, and he won admission to a top-ranked liberal arts school.

Brand: Inventor

Exercise: Inspiring Fire

(30 minutes)

Goal: To find ways to transform adversity into triumph

Instructions: Think of all the ways you've either faced adversity or experienced challenges for being different. Rather than looking at these as negatives, look for ways to transform them into points of pride. You can celebrate your differences through action, service, social awareness, and community-building. With help from parents or mentors, you can transform setbacks and challenges and inspire others to do the same.

22

HARNESSING FIRE:

scaling upwards

HOPEFULLY BY NOW, you're getting a strong sense of what you truly love and where you get the most satisfaction in life. We want you to take your unique experiences and keep building on where your passions are.

As you continue growing the fire inside, you will find that it lights a vision for the life you want in the future. As you do the things you love, you hear a calling, or vocation, inviting you to explore the path further. When you do, you are well along the path of your heroic journey.

Don't stop! Don't look back. Keep going, step-by-step, solidifying your vision of who you are and the life you want to have in college and beyond. When you do, the later challenges of selecting universities and gaining admission will be an exciting challenge instead of a drudging task.

We want you to take your skill and passion as far as you can. We call this process scaling upwards. Don't let anything hold you back. There are no limits except what your mind can imagine. Scaling upwards means taking experiences and accomplishments and building on them.

- If you've done a research project, won an award or scholarship in a particular area of talent, keep pushing, looking for ways to raise your talent.
- If you've exhibited a meaningful work of art at a local venue, then take it to the next level, national or international.
- If you've started a business, club, or community organization locally, explore opportunities to expand.
- If you have a talent you work on at home or school, see if you can convert that into a community-based business or performance.
- If you've faced adversity or overcome a personal challenge, form a club or outreach program to raise awareness and support.

scaling upwards: third-party recognition

Third-party recognition is a primary method for scaling upwards, and it's not as hard as it looks. With so many negative stories, media outlets—from local papers and TV news to online media—are hungry for positive stories about young people taking initiative and making a difference.

It's great if a student starts a club, but if that club is written up in a newspaper or garners a positive quote from a mayor or civic leader, that achievement is suddenly awarded far more weight and importance. Likewise, if a young person forms an acting group that stages a play, that's great, but that achievement will be far greater if it's written up in the local paper.

Recognition can take any number of forms:

- Getting a research paper or journalistic piece published.
- Getting profiled by TV news or a newspaper for academic and extracurricular successes.
- Getting one's name in the newspaper for starting a community service project or winning a science fair.
- Superlative comments from teachers for academic success.
- Positive recognition from leadership figures.

If the thought of getting attention or being in the spotlight makes you feel uncomfortable, that's okay! Congratulate yourself for being a sincere and authentic person.

At the same time, recognition is not about self-glorification. It's about building something much larger than yourself. Recognition can be used to raise awareness for worthy causes, unify the community, and inspire others to realize what is possible when a person takes action.

With these in mind, third-party recognition becomes a win-win for everyone.

Sharon from Belmont, Massachusetts

High School Label: "Robot Girl"
Sparks: Love of computers, commitment, teamwork
Harnessing Fire: Third-party recognition

When we met Sharon as a sophomore, she spoke of her interest in computer science and engineering. Working with her parents, we explored ways that she could develop leadership skills in the field. During her sophomore year, she began pursuing opportunities through tech clubs and science fairs, and got involved in her school's Robotics Team. By her junior year, she'd earned the respect of her teammates and was chosen to lead the team. Dedicating herself to her passion, she coached her team in the invention of a brand new prototype robot, and earned a series of victories at science contests at the state, national, and ultimately international level.

A national magazine wrote up her achievement in an article celebrating youth in science, and her work garnered further recognition through a national "Women in the Sciences" award. She also earned a prestigious scholarship to attend the University of Southern California.

Brand: Robotics Developer

Exercise: Third-Party Recognition

(30 minutes)

Goal: To make sure your hard work and achievements get the validation they deserve.

Instructions:

1. Take your efforts in leadership, service entrepreneurship, performance, art, writing, research, scholarships, or academic competition and see if you can channel them into:

   • raising awareness for a worthy cause,
   • building community, and/or
   • inspiring and educating others.

2. Get your work profiled or published in print, television, or online media.

3. If you earn recognition at the local level, scale that recognition upwards to the state, regional, national, and even international level.

scaling upwards: balancing out academic gaps

No one's perfect. Everyone has classes where they don't do so hot. Sometimes, it's even an entire semester or year that we go off track.

The good news is that low grades and test scores don't have to dash your college hopes. By showing the effort and dedication to overcome academic weaknesses, you can fill those gaps and impress colleges with your maturity and commitment.

The first way to fill academic gaps is by strengthening the weak area directly. This can be done through private tutoring, summer school, and university programs. The second way to fill academic gaps is by showing excellence in your academic specialty. At College Match, we have helped a lot of students balance out weaknesses using this strategy.

Be careful, though!

Academic gaps can only be filled by academic excellence, not extracurricular performance.

Extracurricular performance doesn't fill academic gaps. Every year, students try and fail to correct low GPAs with experiences of leadership or community service. While those efforts are commendable, colleges aren't won over by the effort.

Colleges value academic performance before everything else because they want to be certain that if you come to their school, you will not only survive, but thrive. Therefore, you have to prove your commitment to *academics*.

Margaret from Pasadena, California

High School Label: "Mousy Girl"
Sparks: Talented writer, imaginative, funny
Harnessing Fire: Balancing out low grades

Many students are creative, but some take creativity to new levels. When we began working with Margaret, she made it clear that she wanted to pursue creative writing at her dream school, Vassar College. The problem was that Margaret's GPA in math was several points lower than Vassar's cutoff GPA, and because it was already late in her junior year, there was little chance of retaking courses to raise her GPA.

To balance out her low math grades, we had her turn up the heat on her writing cred. First, Margaret compiled a chapbook of poems, short stories, and humor pieces, which she edited into a cohesive manuscript. She then shared her manuscript with her writing teachers and mentors, and she asked them to pass her work along to other writers in the community. Eventually, her chapbook found its way into the hands of a well-known novelist, who loved her work and commented on it with praise, which Margaret listed in her applications under Awards and Honors.

Lastly, we had Margaret send her manuscript to the head of Vassar's English Department and include an excerpt of her best writing in the "Additional Information" section of her application. This did the trick! With enthusiastic support from the Vassar English department, Margaret was able to balance out her low math grades, and she got admitted Early Decision to Vassar.

Brand: Acclaimed Writer

Exercise: Balancing Out Weak Grades

(30 minutes)

Goal: To strengthen any gaps in your academic record

Instructions: Read the book, What Smart Students Know, which can help you learn to thrive in subjects that have given you a hard time. For all classes where you scored a B-minus or lower, meet with teachers and find about ways that you can make up for low scores.

Decide on ways to fill academic gaps through:

- Summer school
- Private tutoring
- University programs
- Academic research projects
- Publishing

Make a plan with your parents to strengthen any gaps. Consult teachers and guidance counselors as needed.

Checklist #1: Fire

Start: Winter of 9th/10th Grade
(As soon as possible thereafter)

- Determine your **core personal and service ambitions**.

- Decide which **transformative paths** fit you best.

- Choose which **transformative experiences** you'd like to pursue.

- Look at ways you can **turn adversity into personal triumph**.

- Maintain a **GPA** of 3.5 or above.

- Buy SAT and ACT prep books and take practice tests.

- Take **pre-SAT (PSAT) and pre-ACT (PLAN) tests**.

- Look for ways to **scale up** your favorite experiences and accomplishments.

- Be sure to **improve** low grades and test scores.

- **Balance out** any low grades that can't be improved with proof of academic excellence in other areas.

PART VII

Sparks

Fire

VISION

Brand

S
T
U
D
E
N
T
S

WE STARTED WITH your unique sparks of talent and ignited a fire of transformative experiences. That fire now lights the way for you to find the college or university that fits you best. Choosing the right one isn't easy. There are hundreds and hundreds of options, all unique in their own way. You'll need all of the vision and self-discovery you've developed thus far.

The college you attend will ultimately create the adult you become. Your life in the decades after college will be shaped by this pivotal choice, which is why we call it the first adult decision of your life.

We want you to feel pride and gratitude for that decision, not regret. The good news is that everything we've done so far has prepared you for this next step: making choices. Your heroic journey of the first half of this book and the discovery of your unique fire has empowered you to do just that. Just as before, the heroic journey is about having the courage to pursue the life you want.

The second half of your adventure awaits.

"My college needs a good football team."

"I'll go where my parents went."

"How's the party scene?"

"What's the magazine ranking?"

"Where do I begin?"

23

CLEAR VISION:
selection pitfalls

BEFORE WE DISCUSS how to choose, we have to take a moment to discuss how **not** to choose. Not to scare you, but nearly half of all college students never graduate, and a third of college students transfer out of their original school, at a great loss of time and money. It happens because students play roulette with their future and get burned.

Students who choose colleges by superficial standards have to live with the disappointment and frustration. We want to spare you that fate and help you avoid the mistakes that cause thousands of students each year to deeply regret the college they chose, students who find themselves so unhappy with their choice that they end up transferring or dropping out.

Here are the three major pitfalls of college selection, the superficial standards that get students in trouble:

- Party reputation
- Sports teams
- Magazine rankings

pitfall #1: party reputation

You've worked hard in high school, and college promises fun times. Haven't you earned that much?

Yes, you have. But keep something in mind.

The legendary party scenes of movies, magazines, and TV shows usually aren't told by people who passed out vomiting on a bathroom floor, got addicted to drugs, caught an STD, or were sexually assaulted.

Those ugly realities are also a part of party scenes, and college administrators have long since cracked down on them. They've seen one too many drinking deaths, drunk-driving accidents, hazing deaths, and sexual assaults, and they don't want you to be next. These are the party realities that beer and liquor ads forget to put in their disclaimers, and universities don't care one bit about quashing your good times to save student lives and their reputations. At this point, you may be thinking, "I'll take my chances."

That's fine. Just realize that if beer pong, keg stands, and jello shots seem to be a blast your freshman year, you may begin to suffer from Groundhog's Day syndrome.

Repetition. Equals. Boredom.

By sophomore or junior year, those parties won't be so much fun anymore. When you're lying in bed, nauseated with another hangover, wondering what you're going to do with your life, unmotivated by your coursework, you may wonder what might have happened had you chosen a school that you felt truly engaged by.

pitfall #2: sports teams

If choosing a college by party reputation is problematic, choosing for the football or basketball program is equally so. Yet each year, thousands of students choose to select their future lifestyle based on the quality of the sports teams, for reasons that have nothing to do with athletic scholarships.

It's understandable. It's fun to be part of a legendary winning tradition that you've watched on TV all your life. Victory in a packed football stadium or basketball arena can be a blast, with the band playing and the team coming back for the win.

But how do a handful of moments compare to decades of the life you live thereafter? When you're nearing the end of college and the **real world** is growling at you like a 300-pound linebacker, what would you rather have: bowl games and sweet-sixteen appearances or a rock solid preparation for life?

pitfall #3: magazine rankings

One of the biggest mistakes students make is choosing their destiny based on the number rankings given by magazines like *US News & World Report*. Unlike sports rankings, which are based on contests with clear winners and losers, college rankings are based on a random collection of standards that shed no light on whether an undergraduate experience is right for you.

They might as well be ranking ice cream, proclaiming that vanilla beats out chocolate and strawberry, with rocky road and butter pecan tied for fourth place. If you're a Cherry Garcia or pistachio gelato kind of person, what good does vanilla do you? If you choose by the #1 status, you'll end up spending four years with a flavor you don't even like, all because of a magazine ranking.

S
T
U
D
E
N
T
S

Forget about what's "best," and pay attention to what's **right**.

Status is attractive, but we're not talking about a weekend fling. College is a long-term relationship that will stay with you for the rest of your life. Don't get stuck with a school you have nothing in common with, just because they have status.

Find a place that cares about its students, that promises you great career training or preparation for graduate school, that returns the costly investment of time and money. Find the place where your fire will grow, where you will deepen your talents and passions, so that when all is said and done, you'll look back with profound gratitude at the transformation college gave you.

DATING BREAK
Who Do You Love?

Famous schools are like movie stars. They look gorgeous in photographs and you've heard stories about how great they are. From a distance, they seem perfect in every way.

If you had the chance to date a movie star, you'd jump at the chance. Who wouldn't? But would you commit to a four-year marriage? Before driving to Beverly Hills, consider the following:

What will you get from this relationship, beyond the hype, when you're waking up with that movie star day after day? If you only choose by looks and status, you might find that you're just a number to that movie star. They're too busy worrying about their fame and glory to care what you want out of life. Deep down, that movie star is shallow and insincere and treats you terribly. Unfortunately you're married now, and it's a lot harder to get out once you're already in.

The point is, you can choose the famous names, but if you look closely, you'll find amazing and unique schools which will love you for who you are and help you become the person you could only dream of being.

And when you get down to it, that is what love is all about.

dating tip: look for love, not status.

24

FOCUSING VISION:

finding your college type

TO FIND THE right college, you need categories that help you find your unique type.

Magazine rankings are basically useless when it comes to finding the right school, and part of that is because they use descriptions like National, Doctoral, and Regional, which has nothing to do with an undergraduate education.

You need to make an informed choice. You need categories that fit your needs. The descriptions below tell you the kind of experience you can expect, the type of student who is best served by each type, and the kinds of careers each type best prepares its students for.

We break undergraduate schools down into the following six categories:

- Specialty Schools
- Research Universities
- Polytechnics/Land Grant Universities

- Liberal Arts Colleges
- Hybrid Universities
- Teaching Colleges/Comprehensives

As you read the descriptions that follow, explore which types best match who you are and what you want to get out of college.

Specialty Schools

Recommended to:
Students who wish to be career-ready right out of college in the fields of engineering, business, technology, science, design, or the performing arts, and seek training in a highly competitive environment before entering the workforce.

Size
Small—between 500 and 3,000 students.

Description
Specialty schools offer intensive professional preparation in a particular field. Students build portfolios of training experience to offer future employers upon graduation. That said, specialty schools tend to be weak in humanities and social sciences since they focus on one particular field.

Strengths
Excellent job prospects at competitive salaries upon graduation. Strong graduate school placement.

Weaknesses
Lack of well-rounded education.

Specialty Schools by Field
- **Art & Design:** Pratt, RISD, SCAD, North Carolina School of the Arts, Cornish College of the Arts, Cooper Union
- **Performance:** Berkelee, Juilliard
- **Engineering:** Harvey Mudd, Olin, Cooper Union
- **Business:** Babson

Research Universities

Recommended to:
Extroverted and assertive students who won't get lost in the crowd or let large class sizes detract from their educational experience.

Size
Large (10,000) to very large (up to 40,000)

Description
Research Universities are so-named for *doctorate* level research for industries such as defense, technology and pharmaceuticals. So far as undergraduates are concerned, these schools offer famous names and athletic programs, and a variety of majors. **However, classes tend to be held in lecture halls, or are taught by graduate students instead of professors. Due to their size, students at these schools get less personalized attention or mentorship than they would at smaller schools.**

Strengths
Graduating students get recruited by various industries, and assertive students can take advantage of numerous job networking opportunities on campus.

Shortcomings
Less effective at graduate school preparation than liberal arts colleges. Unless you're highly assertive, Research U's offer less personal development, which means your potential doesn't get maximized, and you finish college less prepared than you might otherwise be at a smaller school.

Examples of Research Universities
University of California, Michigan,Wisconsin, Berkeley, Illinois, UNC, Washington, Maryland, Brown, Columbia, Cornell, Dartmouth, Harvard, Penn, Princeton, Yale, Vanderbilt, Duke, Northwestern, Tulane, Stanford, USC, UMass, BU, John Hopkins, University of Chicago.

Polytechnic/Land Grant Universities

Recommended to:
Students who want job preparation in engineering, technology, business, architecture, and agriculture, and who seek a larger learning environment with more course offerings than specialty schools offer.

Size
Large, 10,000 or more undergraduates.

Description
Polytechnics were developed using agriculture and engineering land grants for agriculture. (They often have cows on campus.) Nowadays, they focus on many practical and theoretical fields (hence, *'poly-technic'*) in a variety of courses and majors.

Strengths
Strong professional development in specific programs. While these are usually less competitive at career training than specialty schools, you get more academic variety and an active campus life.

Shortcomings
Polytechnics don't tend to be as strong in grad school placement as liberal arts or small research universities.

Examples of Polytechnics/ Land Grant Colleges
CalPoly, Auburn, Ohio State U, Colorado State U, Oregon State U, Washington State U, Penn State U, Cornell U, UC Davis, Arizona Polytech at Arizona State U, NY Poly, Michigan State, Virginia Polytechnic, Texas A&M, RPI.

Liberal Arts Colleges

Recommended to:
All students who wish to attend grad school. Liberal arts colleges have the best track record for grad school placement and outperform larger research universities in prestigious scholarships like the Fulbright and Rhodes.

Size
Small campuses with student bodies between 500 and 2000.

Description
Liberal arts colleges are small and personalized campuses where students engage closely with faculty and are pushed to express themselves and think critically in a large variety of majors. Class sizes are small and students receive excellent personal attention and mentorship from professors, with opportunities to perform research coauthored by professors.

Strengths
Liberal Arts colleges do an outstanding job of preparing students for elite graduate schools in law, business, and medicine, as well as PhD programs. Many liberal arts colleges have 3:2 joint-programs with Ivy League graduate schools.

Shortcomings
More focused on grad school preparation, Liberal Arts colleges are less geared towards preparing students for careers right out of college. Graduates perform very well, however, in pay scale rankings ten years after college.

Examples of Liberal Arts Colleges
Amherst, Swarthmore, Claremont McKenna, Kenyon, Occidental, Beloit, Hamilton, Grinnell, Amherst, Williams, Wesleyan, Bennington, Whittier, Puget Sound, Whitman, Willamette U, Evergreen State College.

Hybrid Universities

Recommended to:
Students who want to hedge the experience of a research
university and a liberal arts college.

Size
Typically between 2500—6000 undergraduate.

Description
Hybrids straddle the ground between research universities and
liberal arts colleges. They provide some research at the graduate
level and some focus on writing, critical thinking and public
speaking. The Catholic Loyola's are perfect examples. Smaller
research universities that offer higher professor interaction qualify
for this category.

Strengths
Hybrids tend to have better job placement than Liberal Arts, by
offering strong regional job networks. Hybrids also afford students
more personal attention from professors than is possible at large
research universities.

Shortcoming
Hybrids don't perform as well as the Liberal Arts in getting students
into grad school, though elite hybrids are an exception to this rule.

Examples of Hybrids
Santa Clara, Seattle University, University of Denver, University of
Redlands, Loyola Marymount University, Villanova University, Elon
University, James Madison University, Creighton, Gonzaga,
Chapman University, University of Portland, Pacific Lutheran, Regis
University, Fairfield University, Bentley University, Ithaca College,
Alfred University, University of Dallas.

Teaching College/Comprehensives

Recommended to:
Students seeking credentialing programs for jobs, such as teaching
K-12 in a specific state.

Size
4,000 to 20,000 undergraduate.

Description
These colleges were originally set up to educate pre-K-12 teachers.
In recent decades, many teachers colleges have added other fields
of study, becoming comprehensive in their offerings. A good
example is Arizona State which now offers a communications
school, business program, science and engineering campus and a
well-regarded honors college.

Strengths
Comprehensives offer good credentialing programs and usually
afford students with personalized attention from professors and
smaller class sizes.

Shortcomings
Credentials offered by these schools often do not cross state lines.
These programs tend to emphasize formulaic coursework, with
little room for questioning, challenging, or critical analysis of
accepted methods.

Examples of Teachers Colleges/ Comprehensives
Arizona State U, All California State Universities (Chico, California
State University San Francisco State U, San Diego State U, Central
Washington U, Western Washington U, Southern Illinois U, Bowling
Green, Kent State, Sam Houston State, San Jose State, Western
Oregon State University.

Tips for Choosing Undergraduate Type

Based on your life vision, explore which type of school fits best.

- If you have a singular focus on becoming an engineer, science, art, or performing arts, and want to pursue a career out of college which will require a highly advanced level of training, then look at **Specialty Schools**.

- If you wish to pursue agriculture, engineering, business, or architecture right out of college but want a larger campus with more variety than a specialty school can offer, then research the **Polytechnics**.

- If you're extroverted, assertive, and focused enough that a very large institution will enhance rather than reduce your growth, then look at **Research Universities**.

- If you want an excellent, well-rounded education, strong personal development, and entrance into grad school after college, then refine your search to **Liberal Arts Colleges**.

- If you crave the variety of a research university at a smaller school, then consider **Hybrid Universities**.

- If you're interested in getting credentialed as a K-12 teacher within a particular region, then look at **Teaching Colleges/ Comprehensives**.

Exercise: Your Undergraduate Type

(30 minutes)

Goal: To establish which type of school fits you best.

Instructions: Follow the steps below.

1. Does your dream career require graduate school (law, medicine, business school, MA, MFA, and PhD programs) or do you expect to be career ready directly out of college (engineering, finance, performing arts, credentialing programs, architecture, and agriculture)?

   Choose One: ☐ **Grad School**   ☐ **Career Ready**

2. If your career requires graduate school, think:

   • Liberal Arts Colleges
   • Small (Private) Research Universities

   If you will be career ready directly out of undergrad, think:

   • Specialty Schools
   • Polytechnics
   • Large (Public) Research Universities
   • Hybrids
   • Teaching Colleges/Comprehensives

3. Based on your answers to the previous questions, locate the type of undergraduate experience that can best fulfill your hopes and goals of the life you want after college.

   Optimal Undergraduate Type -

25

ENLIGHTENED VISION:

standards for selection

EVERYONE NEEDS STANDARDS. As hard as you've worked to get here, you definitely deserve them. We're talking about a lifelong relationship and we want you to look back on college with love and gratitude, not regret. To keep the latter from happening, you have to understand the colleges you're applying to and make sure their values match yours.

Think of this as if you are buying a car. Neglect the research, and you may end up with a bumpy ride that breaks down, spewing smoke on the highway while the rest of the world speeds by.

Do the research, and your school will take you where you want to go. We use the following standards for rating schools to help you get there:

- Real World Preparation
- Student Satisfaction
- Campus Culture
- Tuition and Financial Aid

S
T
U
D
E
N
T
S

"Real World" Preparation

Graduate School Placement

Use this metric if grad school is likely in your plans. Schools are rated by the percentage of seniors who earn enrollment into masters, PhD, and professional schools (law, business, and medicine).

Pay Scale *Upon* Graduation

College is an investment in your future. How do the colleges you're looking at rate against one another in the career fields you're interested in?

Pay Scale *Ten Years After* Graduation

This metric offers you an idea of long-term earning potential, and takes into account the benefits of attending graduate school. Often Liberal Arts schools have lower pay scales at graduation, but rank among the highest ten years after graduation.

Reputation in Chosen Field

Explore how strong a particular program is at each school in the areas of expertise that your child wishes to develop for the future.

Study/Internship Programs for Credit

This can be an excellent way for students to learn on the job, gain experience and career development, and build important connections before entering the real world.

Student Satisfaction

Average class size

Small classes mean an engaging classes taught professors versus classes fielded by TAs in large lecture hall or auditoriums. Class size can mean the difference between flourishing through personal relationships or losing focus from the lack thereof. Class size is also a big sign as to how much a college cares about their students' experience, whether they see their undergrads as individuals or numbers. (Note: Some larger private schools hire more professors in order to keep their class sizes smaller.)

Percentage of students who graduate within 4 or 5 years

This important figure reveals how successful a college is in helping its students stay focused on their academic goals. A high percentage of students graduating within 4 or 5 years is a good sign. Beware of schools with lower rates of students graduating on time.

Percentage of freshman who transfer

This figure is an excellent indicator of how happy or unhappy students are at any given college. A significant number of freshmen transfer or simply drop out of college after their first year. Right now, about one third of US college students transfer. Checking the numbers on freshman retention can help you avoid an unhappy experience from the beginning.

Best orientation and first-year transition programs

This determines how a school treats its incoming freshman. The first impression of a school goes a long way to shape a student's educational experience.

Poll current students and recent graduates

Current students and recent grads can provide excellent real-time information on the collegiate experience at a university.

Campus Culture

Institutional mission
Mission statements tell a lot about a college's values. Also read about the original founding and intent. (Wikipedia is a great source for this information.)

Public vs. private
Public schools often have a very different dynamic than private schools. Weigh the trade-offs of both and decide which feels best.

Location
You may want to be in the middle of an urban center or in a small town with only nature for miles. Another consideration is whether the school is located near an economic hub for your particular field, which is often the case in fields such as technology, agriculture, and the performing arts.

Breakdown of student body by majors
What majors are students specializing in? How many departments does the college have, and which departments have they been recognized for? Which departments receive the most funding? How do these answers align with what you want to get out of college?

Diversity on Campus
What is the ethnic, social, and class diversity on campus? How homogenous is the climate in terms of nationality and religion? Is the student body known for being open or close-minded? Does the campus have a reputation for being traditional and conservative, liberal and outspoken, or somewhere in between?

Tuition & Financial Aid

Tuition
Consider the cost of living along with tuition, as certain locations are far more expensive than others. *In-state* public universities are typically less expensive while *out-of-state* publics tend to cost as much as private schools. Private schools often make up for the price difference by offering generous financial aid packages.

Types of Financial Aid Offered
With the already-high price of undergraduate education rising each year, debt is a major concern. You should take financial aid into account for every school you consider. Most colleges offer both need-based and merit-based financial aid. Look for schools that are known for their generosity in this regard.

Merit Aid
At College Match, we pride ourselves on securing merit aid for the majority of our students. 96% of our clients were accepted into the college of their dreams and 92% of our clients won merit scholarships averaging $57,250.

One place to learn how schools stack up is Kiplinger's "100 Best Value Schools," an annual issue including such factors as spending per student, merit-based awards, and financial aid. You can find the latest survey here: http://www.kiplinger.com/tools/colleges/.

Exercise: What are your Mandatories?

(1 hour)

Goal: To compare prospective schools side by side.

Instructions:

1. Make a table like the one below, and place college names at the top.

2. On the left, list the standards that you care about. Use the Internet or college prospectus to find how your schools compare.

Metrics	Colleges				
	College 1	College 2	College 3	College 4	College 5
Tuition					
Ratio of Professors to Students					
Percent Graduating in 4 or 5 years					
Class Size					

Exercise: Create an "I" List

(30 minutes)

Goal: To help you clarify which schools you like best.

Instructions:

1. After comparing dozens of different schools, choose the nine or ten that best suit your unique hopes and goals.

2. For each prospective school, make a list of statements expressing what you like best about the school.

   For example :

   - I like the campus.
   - I like the location.
   - I high student satisfaction rate.
   - I like the generous merit scholarships.

3. Go over your "I" list with your parents or a close mentor. Tell them which schools feel like the best fit, and the ways each school can offer you what you need. Weigh your options, and feel out which schools make the most sense for you.

*"Which school best prepares me
for law school?"*

*"I want a competitive job out
of college."*

"Is the campus vibe positive or not?"

*"How much financial aid can
I earn?"*

*"Which college offers the best
program in my field?"*

26

FUTURE VISION:

choosing U

YOU'VE FOUND THE schools that fit you best. You can envision your passions and talents burning brighter on their campuses. You feel an excitement about going there.

Keep going, just a little further. Narrow down your list to the schools you feel most intrigued by. The excitement you feel (or don't feel) will come across in your applications, and it will make a huge difference when colleges sense how invested (or ambivalent) you are about attending their school.

So keep going with these final steps to solidifying your choices.

choosing U: tier by admission chances

It's good to have fallbacks, to cast a wide net of schools, all of which match your vision and personality. We recommend selecting at least nine schools to apply to. That might sound like a lot and it does take effort, but remember, that effort will last you a lifetime.

We begin by tiering the schools by your chances of getting in, making sure you have two or three schools represented in each tier:

- **Super-reach schools** (less than 10% chance of getting in)
- **Reach schools** (10-25%)
- **Fifty-fifty schools** (50%)
- **Safety schools** (>75%+)

These tiers are a combination of the selectivity rating of the schools you're applying to and your personal academic and extracurricular performance. Therefore, the tiers are different for each student.

Guidance counselors and professional consultants like College Match can give you quick and helpful guidance in figuring out which schools stack up where.

IMPORTANT: If you're trying for merit-based aid, chances are higher at less competitive schools. Think of it like this: less prestigious schools will pay more to get strong students than highly prestigious schools, which already have thousands of strong students applying to them.

EXERCISE—Tier Your Colleges

(30 minutes)

Goal: To ensure you have favorite schools in each tier

Instructions: With the help of a guidance counselor or professional consultant, make sure that you have a collection of super-reach, reach, fifty-fifty, and safety schools, to ensure that at each level, you will both feel good about your choices and avoid getting rejected altogether.

choosing U: conduct student interviews

Interviews allow you to take charge of your search and become personally and emotionally invested in the schools you've chosen. You want to know first-hand what students on campus are like and how they feel about their school. Interviews will keep you from going to the wrong college and help you find the right match.

Interview students of each school, particularly in your field of interest. Each student will have a unique opinion, but you'll likely find that recurring themes keep popping up. Maybe the students feel that the professors are really engaged and supportive, or you might find out that students are protesting the way the administration treats them.

Listen closely to what they say! Listen closely to how their answers make you feel. Does what you hear and feel make you want to fill out an application or run the other way?

Trust your intuition.

EXERCISE—Interviews

(30 minutes)

Goal: To ensure you'll love the schools you've chosen

Instructions: Call or email schools' admissions offices. They'll provide student contacts in the fields of study you're interested in. Look at it like detective work. The more you do it, the more exciting the search becomes.

choosing U: campus visits

Once you've narrowed down your list to the schools that you feel highly intrigued by, try to get a real-time experience at those campuses to make sure you can see yourself there. You don't want to apply blindly and put yourself in the position of a rude awakening. Summer university programs are also a great way to get an extended on-campus experience.

If you make a traditional college visit, try to do so during spring break of your junior year so that you get to see how the campus feels **while there are students present**. One problem with visiting during the summer is that most colleges are empty and lack the vibe you'll experience during the school year.

For any campus visit, make sure to do the following to get the most out of the experience:

- Tour classrooms, dorms, cafeterias, and lab facilities.
- Request an overnight stay through the admissions office.
- Request an interview with the department chair in your chosen field.
- Conduct on-the-spot interviews with five to ten students. These interviews provide you honest information that can help you decide whether a school is right for you.

EXERCISE—College Visits

(30 minutes)

Goal: To ensure your prospective schools feel right for you

Instructions: Call or email school admissions offices and ask to set up a visit. Be sure to ask to talk with students in the fields of study you're interested in. Do the detective work, and have fun!

vision: parting thoughts

Now comes the pivotal moment in your journey: selecting the path your life will take. In great movies and books, this is that moment, late in the story, when heroes commit to what they love, to their core identity, and pursue it with all the fire they have inside.

I encourage all of my clients to do some serious soul-searching before making their final decision. The choice isn't easy, but if you feel profoundly invested in each school you choose, you'll feel the excitement going forward that this is not only the first adult decision of your life, but that you're also ready for it.

Do this and you'll have no problem creating compelling applications. You'll naturally be able to convey the vision of the life you want, and your journey will be nearly complete.

Make that investment now, and you'll look back on this moment with pride for the rest of your life.

Checklist #2: Vision

Start: Fall of 11th Grade

- Complete College Goals Exercise.

- Select the Type of Undergraduate Experience that fits you best.

- Research schools and compare them by standards that matter.

- Create an "I"List to gain a clear picture of the schools you like best.

- Continue SAT prep. When your practice scores are well above the cut-off for your dream schools, sign up to take the SAT.

Start: Spring of 11th Grade

- Tier your prospective schools into super-reach, reach, 50-50, and safety.

- Conduct interviews with at least five students from each prospective college.

- Visit prospective universities, preferably during spring break of your junior year.

- Create a Second round Me-List to gain a clear picture of the schools that feel best to you.

- If you weren't satisfied with your score the first time, retake the SAT.

PART VIII

Sparks

Fire

Vision

BRAND

ONE PIECE REMAINS in the journey: admissions.

This final part requires all of the knowledge and skills, the passion and purpose you've gained along the way, as well as all your growth and insight.

The good news is that all along, without even knowing it, you've been developing the ultimate tool for admission. Every time you took chances and stretched your boundaries; every time you showed strength and courage, leadership, and service; and every time you learned from your mistakes and overcame your personal limitations, you increased your chances of admission and winning merit money.

The tool is something I've time-tested tool and have been using for seventeen years to get nearly all of my clients into their top-choice schools, with ample financial aid. We call this tool the Brand because it conveys your unique fire through an ironclad statement of identity, so that rather than just sending in an application and hoping for the best, you'll be using your strengths and experiences to command from a position of power. You'll proudly state to the colleges of your choice, "This is who I am."

Do this and you won't have to worry about rejection. By taking control of your destiny and your purpose, you'll gain acceptance into the life you want to live.

27

CRAFTING THE BRAND:

making your Muv

DO YOU REMEMBER the last boring movie you saw? No?

That's the thing about boring material. It's quickly forgotten.

When you consider that colleges get thousands of applications, you definitely want your application to be memorable. The way to make a memorable application is *not* by piling on an endless list of activities or adding gimmicks or bluffs. College admissions officers are trained to read through all of that, and the second they catch a whiff of insincerity, they move on to the next candidate.

So, how *do* you stand out against the competition? The way you stand out is that core value we've been cultivating from the very beginning: **uniqueness.**

The way you convey uniqueness is the Muv Statement, which stands for *Message of Unique Value*. When admissions officers read your application, the Muv Statement plays out like the theme of a great movie, unifying all of the elements into one meaningful message.

A college application only gives you a small space to make your mark, so everything you put down has to be tied to this one compelling message. Your Muv Statement harnesses the fire of your academic and extracurricular experiences and helps forge them into a memorable brand. It's a mark of maturity that savvy admissions officers notice immediately.

Read the examples from Martin, Chad, and Jessica, and notice how the *Muv* statements create a clear picture of who this student is and how each one is prepared to thrive at college.

You may have never met these three students, but after reading their Muv Statements, you'll know exactly who they are and what they're driven to accomplish in life.

Martin Barlow—Uniquely Daring

Accomplishments
State Bike Racing Champion
3.5 GPA academic achievement
Published article in local paper, "How Racing Made Me a Better Student."
Member of Volunteer Medical Assistance Team in Haiti

Muv Statement:
"Martin Barlow brings the same daring and talent that makes him an award-winning cyclist to his academic studies and volunteer work, taking bold risks to make the world a better place."

Chad Phipps—Uniquely Able

Accomplishments
3.78 GPA

Won his division at the county science fair

Started a club for fellow wheelchair-bound students

Was featured on the local news

Muv Statement:
"Chad Phipps hasn't let the fact that he's wheelchair-bound slow him down one bit, dedicating himself to academics and scientific achievement and helping fellow students with disabilities get the most out of life."

Jessica Stemmler—Unique Excellence

Accomplishments from beginning of 9th grade to present:
4.0 GPA

Lead Trainer at local Stables

Three-time 4H Competition Champion

Summer study, Large Animal Medicine, UC Davis

Muv Statement:
"Jessica's standard of excellence has made her a top student, champion rider, and skilled trainer, motivating her to apply her talents and experience through serving in the field of large animal medicine."

Exercise: Making Your Muv

(30 minutes)

Goal: To convey your fire through a Message of Unique Value.

Instructions:

1. What value best describes your passion for life? (For example, a passion for service, a driven leader, or a quality like determined.)

2. List the experiences that best reveal this driving purpose. How do you hope to lead, serve, or create?

3. Compose a statement which best combines the previous three elements into a message of unique value you offer the world. Brainstorm several drafts until you have a concise, ironclad theme to move forward with.

28

FIRING THE BRAND:

admissions power

A COLLEGE APPLICATION is pretty straightforward. The same basic blanks, lines, boxes, and squares allotted for educational data, test information, academic honors, and extracurricular activities. Most students just fill out the application with little thought, never imagining that someone on the other end is getting thousands of applications that look just like theirs, at least at first glance.

As hard as getting into college has become, students need an extra edge, and this is the hidden secret you can exploit to your advantage:

Colleges are really insecure.

Colleges have weaknesses, and they're terrified of those weaknesses hurting their reputation. If you can find those weaknesses and fill a college's need, **you'll be irresistible to that school.**

admission power: find the college's needs

Notice how hard college brochures work at self-promotion. Just like everyone else, they have a certain image they're trying to project. Your job is to see through the hype and publicity and find out where a college prides itself, where it's weaknesses are, and how it's trying to improve its reputation

Here's where to start.

Where to Find a College's Weaknesses

1) College Review Sites/Internet Research
Find out how the college tries to present itself, where it's trying to improve its reputation, and where it has less-than-positive marks. Hear directly about each college's weaknesses from the current students who attend the college.

2) Interviews with Students and Administrators
There's nothing like on-the-ground information. Often, these people know best where a college needs development. Interviews can give you insight as to where your strengths could be most valuable to the school.

3) University Websites
The typical university website can be daunting at first, but stick around, visit it a few nights in a row, and you'll start seeing the ways the college is trying to present itself and appeal to the public.

4) College Prospectus Books
New editions are published each year. Often, they'll list where a school is expanding or growing, and where it has low ratings or a not-so-positive reputation.

> ## Exercise: Finding the Colleges' Needs
> (1 hour x 3 nights)
>
> **Goal:** To find the key gaps that you can fill at your top choices
>
> **Instructions:** For each of your top choice schools, find weaknesses or unmet needs using the format below.
>
> University Name: _____
>
> Ways the school can/wants to improve its image: _____

admission power: fill the college's needs

All colleges have shortcomings they want to fix and bona fides they want to improve in areas such as diversity, academic reputation, campus unity, and competitive edge. All you have to do is find those needs at your favorite schools and fill them with the skills of leadership, service, creativity, and entrepreneurship that you've cultivated so far.

When you get to the application, you'll want to use every single opportunity you can to communicate the values that can fill colleges' needs in your essays, short answers, portfolios, and letters of reference, all to prove your value at filling colleges' unmet needs.

Julia from San Francisco, California

Julia's Unique Value: Proven Achievement in Science
College Need: More Women Represented in Science
Julia's Smuve: Proven Excellence and Leadership in Science

Julia had many strengths as a student, among them a talent for scientific study. Her sophomore year, she performed an internship at a biomedical research institute, and entered an Intel Science competition. Among her other strengths were leadership, service as class president at her school, and tutoring fellow students in math and science.

When she began researching different universities, we found numerous gaps, especially ones involving women in the fields of science and math. Combining her passion for science and leadership, along with other skills, Julia made a fantastic candidate and was admitted to Whitman College with a scholarship of $15,000 a year.

Stephen from Los Angeles, California

Stephen's Unique Value: Marketing Genius, Skilled Organizer
College Need: More LGBT Representation
StephenGBT Repre Proven Community Bridge Builder

Though we typically work with undergraduate admissions, Stephen contacted us trying to get into business school. While in undergrad, Stephen had led organizations that unified LGBT communities on campus and raised awareness nationally for gay and lesbian struggles. After college, he helped LGBT businesses gain online presence through creative marketing strategies. Working with him, we explored different MBA programs and found that while most mentioned enhancing racial diversity, very few discussed LGBT diversity. Sensing a gap, Stephen utilized his marketing and bridge-building skills and made sure his application and essay echoed his theme of "diversity," and effort that earned him scholarships from USC Marshall and University of Miami.

Exercise: Filling the College's Needs

(30 minutes)

Goal: To be an irresistible candidate to your favorite school.

Instructions:

1. Make a table like the one below.

2. For each college you're applying to, write out each college's weak spots you discovered from your research. Then, going through your points of difference, relative to other applicants, try to pinpoint the strengths you have which can help that particular school to fill its gaps.

COLLEGE NAME	THE COLLEGE'S WEAK SPOTS	YOUR STRENGTHS / EXPERIENCES THAT FILL THE GAP

29

POWERING THE BRAND:

finding your Smuve

A COUPLE OF chapters back, we talked about making your Muv and including one resounding theme in all of your applications. Now, we're going to take your Muv one step further and tailor it to each school you're applying to in a way that fills that college's needs.

We call this unique value exchange, and it means that for each individual application, we're going to turn your *Muv* into a *Smuve*. Your Smuve is a **Strong message of unique value exchange**, and it is the ultimate tool for getting you into college!

Here's the idea:

- Your *Muv* is a personal statement of unique identity.
- Your *Smuve* shows how your unique identity fills the needs of a particular school.
- The *Muv* shows how you'll be a standout at any college.
- The *Smuve* shows how you'll be *perfect fit* at each school.

By spotlighting value exchange on each application, colleges will want you badly. You *will be get acceptance letters* and there will likely be offers of merit aid enclosed. Why? Because working your Smuve convinces admissions officers that:

- You're highly committed to their school.
- You'll thrive on their campus.
- You offer talents that strengthen their university in ways *no one else can.*

Exercise : Finding Your SMUVE

(30 minutes)

Goal: Convert your *Muv Statement* into a *Smuve Statement*.

Instructions:

1. For each of your top choice school, write out their particular needs and the ways you can fill those needs.

2. For each school, shape your *Muv Statement* to capture the ways you fill those needs through Value Exchange. This is your *Smuve Statement.*

30

STAMPING THE BRAND:
strategic application

strategic application: the essay

Applications give you just one chance to express to colleges why they need you at their school: the essay. After grades and test scores, the essay decides the fate of your application more than anything else, so you want to make it count.

Great essays are full of passion and emotion and convey your fire for learning in living color, with vivid details about your heroic path and the challenges and obstacles you've overcome. Generally, colleges have two types of essays: the main essay and supplemental essays (most private colleges and some public use the Common Application).

1. **Main Essay**

   The same essay goes for *all of your colleges.*

   The main essay is built around your *Muv.*

2. Supplemental Essay

You tailor the supplemental to *each college*.

The supplemental is built around your *Smuve*, to express why you're a great fit for that particular college.

For both essays, avoid gimmicks or bragging. Neither will get you far. The winning path for the main essay is to build on your unique value, to stamp your brand with a riveting glimpse of whom you are and why you matter.

Colleges will give you several prompts. If you feel strongly about one of the given prompts, go for it! But if the prompts feel stilted or uninteresting, your response might sound the same. Instead, bring to life the most compelling story you have and tie it back to the prompts.

Give the essay your sincere and authentic best, and use the exercise that follows for guidance.

Exercise: Essay Preparation

(1 hour)

Goal: To convey your unique fire through the essay

Instructions:

1. Look at the essay topics of your applications, and choose the one that most inspires a sense of excitement and passion, the one that best allows you to express your *Smuve*.

2. Set a timer for 20 minutes, and write until it goes off.

3. Read over what you wrote for 10 minutes, taking in what you think works and doesn't work.

4. Again, set a timer for 20 minutes, and rewrite from scratch, honing in on your theme of unique value exchange.

5. Proofread and edit, then give to parents and mentors for feedback.

strategic application: personalize each application

Colleges notice when they're getting treated like a number, and they don't appreciate it. Every school expects to be treated—and needs to be treated—like your first choice. Tailor your responses for each school.

In the steps that follow, we'll show you how. Uniqueness is how you get in. Sadly, most students throw too much information into the application which makes it boring to read, like a bunch of six-hour movies.

The other major mistake is that students copy and paste the same template for every college they're applying to. What's true for dating is true for admissions. You have to make the colleges feel special, and you can make colleges take notice by doing one simple thing.

Personalize.

Personalize each application so that you lead with the strengths that highlight your *Muv* and your *Smuve*.

What we mean is this: let's say a student wins five awards in high school. In no particular order, they are:

- Varsity Football Team Manager
- Photography Portfolio Award, grand prize runner-up

- Perfect attendance record
- "Creative Rising Star" award from the local paper
- GPA ranked 4th in class

In random order, this list doesn't offer a clear thematic vision of who this student is. Ordering achievements in such a way is a waste of crucial space. But by approaching this list strategically, these same accomplishments can be arranged to create a compelling argument of value exchange.

Imagine this student is applying to a Division I school that's trying to improve its cultural reputation. This student could personalize a message of **artistic** value exchange by using the following order:

- Photography Award, grand prize runner-up
- "Creative Rising Star" award from the local paper
- GPA ranked 4th in class
- Perfect attendance record
- Varsity Football Team Manager

What if, on the other hand, the student is applying to a Division III school that has just started a football program and is actively seeking students that can help build the program? In that case, the value exchange could look like this:

- Football manager of the year
- Sports Photography Award, Grand Prize Runner-up
- GPA ranked 4th in Class
- Recognized by Local Paper, Creative Rising Star
- Perfect Attendance Record

This order helps the student fill the Division III college's needs, emphasizing valuable experience in both assisting and promoting a sports program.

Whatever you do, always lead with what you feel are your strongest accomplishments, the strengths that best communicate your *Muv* and *Smuve*.

Exercise: Tailor the Apps

(1 hour)

Goal: To tailor the applications for each school

Instructions:
1. Go through the Points of Difference list.

2. Make a Points of Difference page for each prospective school. Remember, your points of difference should specify where your strengths might stand out the most, relative to other applicants at each college

3. On each page, list the **extracurricular activities, academic honors, and achievements** that best support the value exchange for that school.

4. For the final step, put the lists into an order that most compellingly conveys the message of value exchange.

---

strategic application: stay on message

In successful movies, every scene builds on the main overarching theme. The same is true with successful applications. Anything that clouds the story or muddles the message has to be taken out.

Unfortunately, many students pile on too much information, hoping that it will make them appear more accomplished. They do so much good work, but then, at the last minute, flee from their message out of fear it's not good enough.

It's an understandable mistake, but a costly one. Admissions boards get stacks and stacks of applications every day. They have too much to read already. By staying on message, you'll make sure that your value shines through the entire application. Admissions reps will surely take notice, no matter how worn out they may be.

The exercise that follows will help you do just that.

Exercise: Make Every Space Count

(30 minutes)

Goal: To make sure that everything on the application serves a purpose.

Instructions:
Check your applications to make sure that all information adds to your *Muv* and *Smuve*. Remove any information that clouds those messages.

Notice below how the clubs on the left cloud a message of value while the ones on the right accentuate it.

Delete	Add
Twilight Fan Club	National Finance Contest Winner
Justin Timberlake Fan Blog	All-State Medal Math Team
	Captain, High School Math Team
	All-City Girls Volleyball

strategic application: address weak spots

If you have academic weak spots, either low test scores or a lower-than-B average in any class, you'll want to:

1. **Explain factors that caused the low score.**
2. **Show the proactive steps you took to improve.**

Applications provide you with a place to explain factors that might have caused you to get low grades and scores. **It's very important, however, not to complain or blame anyone else—especially a teacher—for your low marks.** That's very un-heroic, after all.

All you want to do is state in an honest and mature way that you acknowledge any valid reasons why you got a low grade. If you're in doubt as to what are valid and invalid reasons, use the following tables.

Valid Explanations	Invalid Explanations
+ Learning disability	- Lousy teacher
+ Language barriers (for immigrants)	- Didn't like subject
+ Serious medical issues	- Light medical ailments
+ Socio-economic challenges	
+ Family challenges	

If you don't have a good reason why you didn't get a good grade, that's okay. Maybe you weren't serious about academics that year. Maybe you just aren't strong in the subject.

Regardless, it's important here to show that you made a strong effort to improve the areas where you got low scores. Maybe you got a tutor, retook the class, or attended extra prep classes. You did your best. You just didn't do quite well enough. For any low scores, that's an explanation the that a university needs to see.

S
T
U
D
E
N
T
S

Exercise: Explain Low Grades and Scores

(1 hour)

Goal: To make sure any low grades or test scores are spoken for

Instructions: For any classes where you scored below a 3.0 GPA or had below-average test scores, explain in the application what caused the score and list the efforts you made to improve. You want to provide a mature message that takes responsibility, and shows your willingness to learn from setbacks.

strategic application: early application

If you have your heart set on a school, early decision is a good way to go, especially if that school is a Super Reach or Reach. Before you leap, be sure you understand how the methods of early application work.

1) Early Decision

When you apply by **early decision** to a school, you're making a morally binding agreement that if you get accepted, you'll go there and nowhere else, even if you get accepted to a "better" option.

Only use **early decision** for your dream school. If you aren't sure it's your favorite, wait for regular decision. The only reason to turn down an early decision acceptance would be for financial reasons, such as if you didn't receive the financial aid needed to attend. Apart from that, you're pretty much are locked in. While it is possible to get out of the agreement—it isn't legally or financially binding—you'll burn bridges at that institution.

2) Early Decision *Two*

Some private colleges now allow a second round of early decision applicants, meaning that if you don't get into your first choice early decision, you can try again through **early decision two**, if you feel your chances are better.

3) Early Action

A lot of schools have begun offering **early action**. Early action is basically like early decision, except that it isn't binding in any way. You are essentially applying early to let that university know that they're at the top of your list.

4) Restricted Early Action

Like early action, **REA** isn't binding, but the restricted part means that you agree not to apply early admission anywhere else (Stanford is one school that uses REA).

Exercise: Applying Early

(1 hour)

Goal: To decide if you should apply early

Instructions: If you have a dream school that you like above all the rest, look into your options for applying early.

---

strategic application: letters of recommendation

Most private colleges want two letters of recommendation. Public schools vary, from two recommendations to none at all. Be sure to check college admissions websites for information.

You want your recommendations to highlight your *Smuve*, the key skills and accomplishments that underline the unique value exchange you offer each university. Think of it this way: colleges will read your applications and your *Muvie* will play in their heads.

When the teachers, coaches, and mentors send their letters, those recommendations will cement your themes of unique value.

Colleges like to see letters from one humanities teacher (English, history, or the arts) and one math or science teacher. If you can, go with this combination.

Ask your letter writers at least two months before your applications are due. Three months is even better. After receiving agreement to write your letter, you want to provide your letter writers with a **Helper Sheet**, which contains your Muv Statement and the accomplishments and experiences which support the message of unique value that you're going to stamp your applications with. Teachers and other mentors are very busy already, and a helper sheet will ensures that your letters support the theme of your unique value.

Lastly, make sure that your letter writers are enthusiastic about helping you.

Ask them if they'll write you a *strong letter of recommendation*. If they seem the slightest bit hesitant, find someone who is enthusiastic to write your letter.

Exercise: Letters of Recommendation

(1 hour)

Goal: To make sure you receive strong letters of support

Instructions:

1. Check university websites to see if prospective schools require Letters of Recommendation, and if so, how many they require.

2. At least two months before application deadlines, approach potential references and ask if they'd be willing to write an **enthusiastic** letter. If there is any hesitation, find someone who will write an enthusiastic letter.

3. Provide each reference with a Helper Sheet to ensure that letters highlight application themes of unique value with supporting achievements.

strategic application: final thoughts

Rejection isn't the end of the world. At the beginning, we said that the most important acceptance you can get is from yourself. If you use high school to discover who you are and what you love, if you pursue your talent and passion with excitement and courage, and embrace your uniqueness through paths of service, leadership, and creativity, you'll discover what no one else can give you and no one can take away: you.

If you let your vision guide you to the right schools and stamp your applications with a branded statement of your unique value, the right college will embrace you, and you'll have the means to begin a new hero's journey of self-discovery.

Regardless of what the colleges decide, you'll have the memories, the most important stories of all, to remind you of the talents and skills you bring to this world.

We wish you well on your journey.

ABOUT THE AUTHOR

David Montesano,
Founder of Montesano Method

DAVID MONTESANO IS a leading college admission strategist. Profiled by *Washington Post* education writer, Jay Matthews, in *Newsweek*'s 2005 edition of *America's Hottest Colleges*, David Montesano was called one of the "new breed of college admission consultants who use business school marketing principles to sell students to their preferred college."

David's work and publications give students and their families clear direction on how to apply successfully to their first-choice colleges, including ways students can identify their unique value and message, the process of differentiation, and the importance of using "The Message of Unique Value" philosophy. Leveraging the techniques, tips and tools learned from 18 years of helping students gain admission to their first-choice colleges, David has created The Montesano Method, a groundbreaking process through which students determine their life goals and position themselves for admission to the college of their dreams. With the Montesano Method, students and their parents can finally gain control over—and actually enjoy—the undergraduate application process.

David's results speak for themselves. Over the past 13 years, 96% of Montesano Method students have gained admission to their "reach" colleges and graduate schools. Moreover, David's students have won merit scholarships averaging $57,000 over four years, the largest amount among students whose awards are being measured.

Brand U: 4 Steps to the College of Your Dreams is David's second book; he is also the author of *10 Strategic College Admission Steps*, published by College Bound News. David contributes to *The New York Times, U.S. News & World Report's "Best Colleges," CBS Moneywatch, Seattle Magazine,* and *Newsweek/Daily Beast*. Additionally, he has appeared on CBS-TV, Fox and made regular appearances on national radio shows and webcasts, including *College Week Live*.

ACKNOWLEDGEMENTS

I OWE A huge debt of gratitude to the families I have worked with over the past two decades. My students and their admission stories are the centerpiece of this book. Without their commitment and dedication, there would be no *Brand U*. I would also like to thank the following colleagues who made this book possible:

Co-author Charlie Mandell, a great wordsmith and friend who made the re-working of this book not only possible, but fun as well; Alejandro Moreno, who tirelessly edited and verified this book's data and statistics; and Chris Morda, who fashioned the book's manuscript into readable text.

I would also like to thank CBS MoneyWatch's education writer, Lynn O'Shaughnessy; college guidebook author, Donald Asher; and former Monster.com executive, John McLaughlin for their feedback on early versions of this book.

This book is dedicated to the late college admission guru Loren Pope, author of *Colleges That Change Lives* and *Looking Beyond the Ivy League*, a friend and mentor early in my career.

CPSIA information can be obtained
at www.ICGtesting.com
Printed in the USA
FSOW03n1210150716
22794FS